I0223085

LINGER

365 Days of Peaceful Pauses

Karyn Henley

Andon Press
Nashville

Linger: 365 Days of Peaceful Pauses

www.KarynHenley.com

ISBN 978-0-9986292-8-5 (pbk), 978-0-9986292-9-2 (epub)

INTRODUCTION

The three-story, boxy building was ages old. The wooden floors creaked. The halls smelled like polished wood, floor wax, books, and kids—and on a lucky day, chili for Frito pie. I was in eighth grade and on a mission to complete an English assignment: Go to the school library and check out a book in a different section from where you usually choose a book. The floor creaked as I entered the otherwise silent library. Usually I'd head straight for the fiction shelves, but I paused. Where to now?

Straight ahead was as good a direction as any, so I tiptoed to the back wall and found myself in the section that held nature nonfiction. I scanned the shelves, and when a small book caught my eye, I pulled it out, flipped through it, and decided it would do. And it did. More than I ever expected. It was a diary of sorts about the author's lively backyard, a world of birds and small animals and seasons passing. I don't remember the author's name or the title of the book, but I do remember the feeling the book gave me: wonder.

That was a long time ago. I've been a writer for years, and I don't know why it took so long to circle back to this wonder in my own work. Maybe it's because the floors of my heart have become creaky. I've tiptoed to the back wall and found myself (in more ways than one) in nature. So this is my offering to you: a year's-worth of reflections, a diary of sorts, a meditative conversation, an invitation to linger. Lingering simply means pausing for a minute or two, slowing down long enough to notice the present moment with all our senses. Lingering refreshes me and enriches my soul. I hope these pauses will also enrich your soul and, perhaps, be a gentle guide to your own year of lingering, noticing, and wonder.

Two notes:

First, since I live in the northern hemisphere, I've begun this book with winter. If you live in the southern hemisphere, you may want to start with the summer months.

Second, it may take you more than a year to get through this 365-day guide. No pressure. You can skip some entries and even double back and start again. Or you may be a pro at lingering and find you don't need my input at all. Use this book in whatever way suits you.

WINTER

JANUARY

1. WINTER SKY

The sky is blue, of course.
Unless it's gray or pink or purple
or green-streaked
or golden.
The sky looks wide and boundless.
Until it peeks over the shoulders of skyscrapers
or winks through leafy branches.
The sky is higher than I can reach,
or so I thought
until I realized that, really,
the sky begins at my feet.
Sky weaves around me,
stretches up from the ground
out into wide, boundless space.
I take a deep breath.
I inhale the sky.
– kh –

I'm lingering with the sky today, looking up at a bold blue swept with winter clouds feathered with ice. What is your sky like today? Inhale. Take a deep breath of sky.

2. COLD WEATHER GIFTS

I huddled in my coat, tense and shivering in the freezing outdoor air. My mind tensed, too, as I hurried from one indoor warmth to another across the college campus in Texas, where I grew up. As a warm weather girl, I fought the winter, cringing against the cold, impatient for warmer weather. Even after I learned to ski in Colorado, the best part of a ski trip for me was returning to a toasty warm house at the end of the day. I didn't really stop fighting winter until I spent some time in graduate school in Vermont. In January. Only then did I begin to really pay attention to the beauty of winter: the lace of leafless branches silhouetted against the frosty sky, the grace of evergreens keeping their vigil as the other trees slept, the hilly drifts of pure white snow in yards and on rooftops, and red-cheeked friends accustomed to the cold, laughing and trekking into town through snow showers. The cold air became a snappy wake-up, winter's nippy way of calling me to attend, to be present, to pay attention.

Attend and attention come from the Latin word that literally means to stretch. Lingering is a way of stretching our awareness of the moment. Lady Winter calls us to be aware, to pause, to notice, and to wonder at her gifts.

3. WINTER SCENTS

Crystal winter air
teased by drifting chimney smoke,
rich warm smell of Yes.
– kh –

I caught the whiff of a light floral fragrance when I stepped outdoors today. Was this a winter-blooming flower? An early spring? After lingering with it a moment, I realized that it was the scent of fabric softener dryer sheets drifting from a neighbor's vent. Still, I paused to appreciate the memory of spring past and the foreshadowing of spring to come. To me, the true scents of outdoor winter are chimney smoke and pine. Indoors, it's the aroma of chili pepper and cumin or cinnamon and nutmeg, traditional and comforting. And cocoa, too. Or if I'm in a more energetic mood, an herbal tea. All invite me to linger. But then, so do neighbors' dryer sheets.

4. THE SOUL AJAR

The soul should always
stand ajar, ready to
welcome the ecstatic
experience.
– Emily Dickinson –

The large empty planter pots are upside down on the back porch and stacked like bricks, one on top of two. My youngest grandson calls this his castle. Children are experts at finding wonder in common objects that adults take for granted or rush past without seeing. One of the benefits of spending time with children is noticing the world with fresh eyes. Sometimes even when I'm not with a child, I try to look around as if I were seeing the world for the first time.

Enter a space of childlike wonder. Look. Listen. Taste. Smell. Touch. Hold on to what enriches you. Leave your soul ajar. Make a castle.

5. DIAMONDS OF FROST

> The seasons alter: hoary-headed frosts
> Fall in the fresh lap of the crimson rose.
> – Shakespeare –

Overnight, frost settled on flowerpots, on stair rails, and on the dry brown petals and leaves of the hydrangea. A layer of water on the lid of the sandbox turned into a thin crust of ice as fragile as crystal. Delicately folded and curiously wrinkled, it glinted in the morning sunlight like the facets of a diamond. My world is covered in sun-sparked frost today. I have diamonds in my garden.

6. CLAIM A TREE

The aging hackberry tree in the center of our backyard had to go. Who knows how old it really was. When we moved in almost forty years ago, it was already tall and full. I'll admit that hackberries are not the prettiest trees around. They're certainly not as classy as the towering elm in the southeast corner of our backyard. But I grew up in nearly treeless West Texas, so hackberries, well, they're trees, and they're shady. I would keep them all forever, but this one was diseased and in danger of falling on our house during a windstorm. So, the hackberry went. The tree trimmers climbed high into the topmost branches and began cutting it down, section by section. When they were done, the yard was much sunnier. And surprise! All this time, in the southwest corner of the yard, was another elm tree, a twin to the elm in the southeast corner. It, too, was towering and classy but had been hidden by the hackberry, unnoticed by me. Until now. From my upstairs desk, I no longer look out on a hackberry, but I have a great view of an elm.

Choose a tree that you see often. Take a good look at it today. Then watch it change through the seasons.

7. BLUE NORTHER

[T]he wind blows strong . . .
from the hills where snow must have fallen,
the wind is polished with snow.
– D.H. Lawrence –

Growing up in Texas, I was accustomed to strong winds in every season. When an ice-cold wind would blow in from the north, we called it a "blue norther." Pause and turn your face to the wind today. Is it blustery? Breezy? Barely moving at all? Linger with it a moment before moving on.

8. THE CLEAN-UP PARADOX

Inks, pencils, glue, ribbons, wire, pastels, stencils, scissors, stamps, paints, a variety of papers—all this and more is available for exploring and play at Art & Soul Nashville, the studio I often attend for art classes. A few hours of artistic discovery results in unique, soul-deep creative expressions. It also results in an array of messes to clean up before we can go home. I was never privileged to be in a class taught by the founder of the studio, Arunima Orr, but I was told that when it came to cleaning up, she encouraged everyone to slow down. "Slow down, and you'll get it done faster," she would say.

Slowing down doesn't mean moving at a snail's pace. It simply means easing back on the speed. The paradox is that when I rush, a task often takes me longer, because I have to stop to pick up something I dropped. Or I have to scrub something twice because I missed part of it the first time. Or I have to go back and grab something I forgot. If I slow down just a bit, I become more thoughtful and deliberate, and I often get it right the first time.

When you clean up today, slow down. Just a bit. Linger with it. Notice textures and sounds, scents, shapes, and sizes. See if you get it done in a less frenzied, more thorough way. And maybe even faster.

9. THE SNUGGLE FACTOR

It's a cold night. I'm wearing a sweatshirt to bed and adding a thick, knitted throw to my bed. There's something satisfying and cozy about putting on a sweatshirt or soft, warm sweater in cold weather. Or bundling up in a knitted scarf and thick coat. Or settling under a warm blanket. Or finding comfort under a comforter. I think of it as the snuggle factor. When my mother tucked us in on a cold night, she would say we were "snug as a bug in a rug." (I think it was Benjamin Franklin who actually made up that rhyme in a letter to a friend who had just lost her squirrel—yes, her squirrel.) Anyway, linger with the feel of being held and hugged and warmed. Pay attention to the experience, and enjoy the moment before moving on.

10. ROOFTOPS

Of all the scenes in movies I've seen, the one that most touched my heart with longing and wonder is in *Mary Poppins*. It's the end of the scene in which chimney sweeps dance like acrobats across the rooftops. As the music drifts to a dreamy end, Burt the chimney sweep sings in almost sacred awe, "on the rooftops of London, coo, what a sight." In the deepening twilight, rooftops and chimneys surround Burt as far as the eye can see. I'm lucky that from my upstairs windows, I can see across the roofs of some of the houses in my neighborhood. They're all different in the pitch of the roofs, the gables, the eaves, and the chimneys, some with short, round smokestacks on top, others with rectangular tops that have roofs of their own. What's fascinating to me about rooftops? I'm not sure. They cover and protect. They quietly stand above the busy-ness below. To me, they seem touch-the-sky aspirational. In a way, they feel like prayers. They inspire me to dream.

11. SNOW

Winter's gusty laugh
twirls icy sparkles skyward.
Dance, tiny snowflakes, dance.
– kh –

Snow is the picture postcard of winter, but it was not the norm for me growing up in Texas. When we got snow, it was an adventure. Snow is more common here in Nashville, although it rarely gets very deep. Still, I'm happy to see the drifts of white that protect my plants, unlike ice and sleet, which can destroy them. I love knowing that my spring garden lies hidden and sleeping under a blanket of snow.

Whatever weather you have today, pause and linger with it for a moment.

12. CRADLING A CUP

In his poem "Sunday Morning," Wallace Stevens wrote of "Coffee and oranges in a sunny chair." For me, one of the pleasures of a cold morning is cradling a not-too-hot cup of coffee between my palms, feeling the shape and warmth of the cup, inhaling the aroma, and sipping it black. It's a beautiful way to linger on a Sunday morning. Or any morning, really. Whatever morning drink is your favorite, pause as you hold it between your palms. Feel, smell, sip, and linger with it a bit.

13. THE GRACE OF HOME

Twellen is an old German word that means to tarry. To stay awhile. To linger. It's the root of our word dwell. There are some rooms where we don't want to tarry, even if we have to spend time there. They feel unfriendly or uncomfortable. Then there are places that invite and welcome us, places that feel restful, comfortable, like home should feel. Maybe they are home. One place where I feel at rest is in the main sanctuary of Second Presbyterian Church. It's fairly small as far as church sanctuaries go, but with its vaulted roof and walls of windows, it feels airy and light and inviting. I can sit in a pew, rest within the lines of the room, and feel the grace of home.

Linger in a room that you find friendly and inviting. Notice the lines of the ceiling and walls. Consider the light, the color, the fragrance. Breathe its peace and energy, and carry that with you when you step away.

14. WINTER SHADOWS

On a sunny day,
I look for shadows,
silent shape-shifters
swiftly changing,
sprawling over a lawn,
flowing across a street,

weaving through fences,
falling over a house like an embrace,
now sharp, now fuzzy,
now not there at all.
I watch the way
walls and ceilings bend and block
the light that spills through windows.
I wonder at the way
a shadow's sharp edges soften
in the lowering sun
and melt into the quiet,
dark peace of night.
–kh–

Look for shadows today and linger with them.
Watch them change. If you have time, get a piece of
paper, lay it on top of a shadow, and trace its edges.

15. NIGHT NOTICING

Tonight after I turned off my bedside lamp, I
paused to settle into a restful peace, letting my eyes
linger on the skewed rectangular pattern created by
my neighbor's garage light shining through my
windows. A car passed, and its lights lit the angles of
the dormer ceiling for a moment. Then all settled back
to the grayed tones of the shadows cast by my
windows. When I was a young girl, I often spent the
night at my grandmother's house, which was on the
corner of a busy street. After dark, snuggled in her

king-sized bed, I would watch light flash through the bedroom windows from the headlights of cars turning the corner. Like Tinkerbell, the light splashed one wall, flowed around the room, and then darted back out, chasing the car.

Find a moment to notice the night and linger with it.

16. DRIFTING SOUNDS

I'm listening to the patter of a cold rain against the windows when the timer on the stove beeps, and the toasty smell of a buttermilk waffle calls me. I slip the toasty, dimpled round onto my plate, plop more batter onto the griddle, and close the lid. The waffle-maker clicks as the heat cycles on again, and the batter sizzles into shape.

My knife scritch-scratches butter onto my waffle. I add a handful of blueberries, pour myself a cup of coffee, and breakfast is ready. As I happily crunch and munch, I listen to the sounds drifting in through closed windows. The rain is heavier now. The neighbors' overnight guests, in the process of leaving, scramble to get their gear and themselves into their car before they get soaked. A slam of car doors, the rev of an engine, and they're gone.

The waffle iron clicks off with a bit of a crackle, and I realize I forgot to set the timer. But the waffle is just right, and the butter melts as soon as I spread it.

The cat runs past me, pad-pad-pad across the hardwood floor. And now all I hear is rain.

The clink of silverware. The hum of the fridge. The call of a distant train. The sigh of wind passing through branches. The crunch of dry leaves underfoot. A cat's purr. The world whispers, "Listen. Listen. This is a gift. For you. Today. Listen."

17. WINTER TREASURES

What good is the warmth of summer,
without the cold of winter to give it sweetness.
– John Steinbeck –

Find a bit of winter nature to observe, something to listen to, smell, and touch. It may be as large as the sky or as long as a path through the woods, as small as a brittle fallen leaf or as large as a tree trunk. Linger with it and let it lead you to wonder.

18. BREATH

[T]he whited air
Hides hills and woods, the river, and the heaven . . .
– Ralph Waldo Emerson –

Pause outdoors long enough to breathe winter. What does it feel like where you live? Is it a brisk, wake-up breath? Is it nippy? Sharp? Steel-cold? Are you breathing through a muffler, a scarf, a mask?

Listen to the sound of your breath. If it's a cold day, watch the steam drift from your mouth and turn into part of the sky.

19. NATURE'S PAINTINGS

'Twas a snowy evening.
How many umbrellas went by?
– Hokushi, translated by Asataro Miyamori–

All my windows function as picture frames for me, each one bordering a unique view of nature's paintings, the real, live, ever changing picture that's outside. From day to day and season to season, the picture changes. Even throughout the day, the picture shifts as it's bathed with light and shadow—dawn, midday, clouds, sunset, dusk, moonlit night. Choose a window in your own house or office, and watch nature paint for you day by day. If your view is a nature scene, let it be a sacred space, a small revelation of nature. If your view is a building or other structure, let it be a small tribute to shapes, textures, and shadows. Either way, it's a unique view just for you.

20. STEAM

Too hot to remain liquid,
you gather and rise,

drawn into the embrace
of cooler air
that invites you
into a swirling dance.
You drift upward,
clouding,
swaying,
twirling,
curling,
stretching,
thinning,
spreading,
vanishing.
– kh –

A cup of hot tea, a mug of coffee, a bowl of soup—
they say, "You may think you can drink all of me, but
part of me cannot be contained, for part of me is a
dancer." I blow this dancer and watch it shimmy
before it settles back into an elegant, upward,
vanishing swirl.

21. STARS

We shall find peace,
We shall hear angels,
We shall see the sky
Sparkling with diamonds.
– Anton Chekhov –

The most impressive night sky I've ever seen was in Badlands National Park. That night, my husband and I and our two sons settled onto a quilt in a field surrounded by buttes and bluffs far from city lights. We had gathered with other park visitors to listen to the "Night Sky" ranger talk. As nightfall gradually enfolded the buttes, we all grew quiet and still and even reverent, dwarfed by the immense expanse of the heavens sprinkled with more stars than I'd ever seen in one place. Shooting stars streaked across the sky and vanished. Bright satellites steadily drifted across. Blinking jets sailed the heavens so high we couldn't hear them. We picked out constellations: Scorpio, the Northern Cross, Cassiopeia. Three planets—Jupiter, Mars, and Venus—formed a line, an event that the ranger said happens only once every 2,000 years. And everywhere there were stars, stars, and more stars.

When skies are clear, long winter nights make for good stargazing. If it's a clear night, look up and linger for a moment with the stars.

22. SLOWING THE PACE

Take more time, cover less ground.
– Thomas Merton –

A replay lingers with an action, alters its pace so we can notice it all. Of course, real life doesn't have replays, but we can slow down. Notice what happens when you slow your pace just a bit—not snail-slow, just a beat or two slower—and pay attention to the moment, to your movement through it, to what your senses tell you.

23. ICY SNOW

> Sorry, little birds.
> I did not expect the ice.
> I'll chip it now. Drink!
> – kh –

In our part of the world, while we do have snow, winter is just as likely to bring an ice storm or sleet or at least those little pellets of snow known as soft hail or, technically, graupel. I try to keep a heater in my birdbath so the water won't freeze, but sometimes I'm late plugging it in for the season. Then I have to chip away the layer of ice on top of the water. Sometimes the water is frozen solid. But when the heater is on and the water stays fluid, birds tend to gather in a circle around the edge of the warm birdbath. Today it was ringed with plumped up robins huddling for warmth.

Notice your winter birds, what they do, how they fly or huddle or step along looking for food.

24. COLD DAY, WARM CAT

> When I play with my cat, who knows
> whether she isn't amusing herself with me
> more than I am with her?
> – Montaigne –

The morning is cold, but I have a cup of coffee to warm me from the inside out and a cat on my lap to warm me from the outside in, although I'm sure that from the cat's perspective, I am warming her. She gets quite cuddly when the weather is cold and snuggles next to me in bed at night like a child's stuffed animal. She's soft and smoke gray with a pink nose and white outlines around her sage green eyes. We adopted her from our son who owned a coffee shop, so she's named after a type of coffee: Djimma.

Djimma is perfect to linger with, to touch, to listen to, to watch. I suppose most pets are. They were probably the world's original entertainers—and lap blankets.

25. WINTER FLAVORS

This morning, I had fresh blueberries with my oatmeal, a taste of summer in winter. The real taste of winter, to me, is warm and spicy like cinnamon rolls, hot chocolate, and chili. When I was a child, my mother often set a large bowl outside when it snowed. When the bowl was full, she would make ice cream with the snow. It was sweet, rich with vanilla flavoring, and more icy than creamy. That, too, is a flavor I associate with winter. But today, I'm lingering with the flavor of oatmeal and blueberries. And coffee. I can't forget the pleasure of lingering over a cup of coffee, especially on a cold morning. Linger with a winter flavor today.

26. PENS AND PENCILS

When I was in elementary school, I wrote and doodled with a fountain pen that had ink refills. Now I use a ballpoint pen, mostly for grocery lists and jotting notes to myself. I use a mechanical pencil for crossword puzzles (along with a good eraser). And, because I'm an artist, I have a variety of good pencils from hard lead to soft for sketching. When you next write or draw or doodle, linger with it. Watch the flow of ink or the trail left by the graphite. Feel the strokes. Marvel at how your brain connects with your hand, which connects with your pen or pencil and makes legible marks (or scribbles or doodles) on the surface you're writing on.

27. PATTERNS

The old, gray hackberry tree in our front yard has an eye. It's a knothole, really, but at just the right angle, it makes the tree look like an abstract face. When I linger, I find faces and figures in the bark of tree trunks. I find letters, hearts, and figures in the dark grain of my hardwood floors. On Sundays when I was young, while the preacher preached at church, I would find faces in the pattern of the wood that paneled the walls. And at my grandmother's house, my sister and I would lie on the couch and stare at the ceiling, which was covered in wallpaper with a pattern so busy it wiggled if you stared at it. Patterns invite our imaginations to play. Pause when you see an interesting pattern today.

28. GO OUT TO GO IN

> I only went out for a walk,
> and finally concluded
> to stay out till sundown,
> for going out, I found,
> was really going in.
> – John Muir –

Going out can mean spending time in nature like Muir did. But going out can also mean simply taking a moment to emerge from mentally reliving our memories or pre-living our future, to step out of our busy minds for a moment and ease into the present, tangible world. There's a sense of wonder, a joy, a gratitude that can only be accessed by returning to the childlike practice of experiencing the moment with as many senses as possible. There's a peace that can only be found by lingering and noticing. If you're in the habit, it doesn't take long, just a pause really, a breath or two to take in the moment, to be inspired, to be enriched, to go out to go in.

29. RHYTHMS

Listen to the rhythms of life,
the tap of raindrops or sleet on the windowpane,
chimes blown by the wind,
a repair worker hammering,
a spoon stirring in a pot.
Listen to the birds' call-and-response,
the turn signal clicking in the car,
a broom swishing across the floor.
Listen to footfalls fading away.
Listen to the beat of your own heart.
– kh –

30. STREAMERS IN THE SKY

A distant, low, continuous growl starts softly to the east and grows louder as it nears. I look up to watch for the jet. It tracks northwest across the deep blue sea of sky, leaving in its wake a streamer of white that crosses the trailing line left by a jet heading north only minutes before. To the east, another jet draws a vapor trail headed southeast, parallel to the first but at a higher altitude, which makes its trail appear thinner, especially now that the first trail I saw is fluffing out in a wide drift. My oldest grandson once called these trails "scratches" in the sky, and that's exactly what they look like. Some days there are no scratches, aka vapor trails or contrails (condensation trails). They only form when the temperature and humidity in the atmosphere are just right. Today is one of those days. The skies are busy, people coming, people going. And here below, I linger to watch the white marks they leave behind in their passing.

31. AT AN ANGLE

A white-breasted nuthatch visits my birdfeeder almost every day. I lingered today to watch him dart in and cling upside-down to the outer metal mesh of the feeder. After he glanced around cautiously, he nabbed a seed and flew off. Of all the birds at my feeder, nuthatches are some of the most interesting, because they eat upside down. I wonder if nuthatches have a more expanded view of the world than most birds, because they see it not only from right-side up but from upside-down, too.

As a wiggly child, I twisted and leaned and turned and hung upside-down from couch seats and chair seats and swingsets. In that topsy-turvy position, I pretended I lived in an upside-down house. I imagined walking on the ceiling; to get to the next room, I had to step over the top of the door jamb, which was now no longer the top but the bottom. Like most children, I viewed the world from all kinds of angles that now, as an upright adult, I use only occasionally. It's an interesting way to linger. Angle your head. Look at the world on a slant. Or even upside down.

FEBRUARY

SIGNS OF THE SEASON

If the simple things in nature have a message that
you understand,
rejoice, for your soul is alive.
– Eleonora Duse –

One of my favorite signs of the winter season are the juncos, small slate gray birds that visit only in winter, and the cardinals, their plump red bodies bright against the evergreens. I also love to see red winter berries giving color to the garden along with a mahonia that blooms in late winter with fountain-like sprays of small yellow blossoms.

What's your favorite sign of the season? Linger with it if you can.

2. WINTER BRANCHES

> Leafless branches arch,
> angle, interweave to frame
> cloud veils spun of ice.
>
> – kh –

In the lavender twilight, bare branches of winter become one of nature's most stunning works of art, a silhouette of black lace unique to each tree. I miss leaves, but bare branches against the sky have their own beauty.

Pay attention to this day. Tomorrow's gift will be different

3. BE POKY

> For everything there is a season.
> There is a time for everything under heaven.
> – Ecclesiastes 3, the Bible –

In the full quote from Ecclesiastes, the list includes planting and harvesting, weeping and laughing, being silent and speaking. I might include moving ahead and lingering—or being poky, as my granny would say. *Poky* comes from the word *poke* in the sense of prodding or nudging an animal or person along. So be a bit poky today. Each day opens its palms and offers us gifts of the season. Taste its flavors. Hear its song.

4. DANCE OF FLAMES

> Now stir the fire, and close the shutters fast,
> Let fall the curtains, wheel the sofa round,
> And, while the bubbling and loud-hissing urn
> Throws up a steamy column, and the cups
> That cheer but not inebriate, wait on each,
> So let us welcome peaceful evening in.
> – William Cowper –

My younger son and his Norwegian wife know how to build a fine fire in their fireplace. The comfort of sitting in its glowing warmth in conversation often eases into a quiet, musing reverie, a drowsiness in good company. Fireplace, campfire, candle flame— it's easy to linger there, to get lost in the crackle, the warmth, the aroma, the shifting colors, and the dance of the flames.

5. FROM THE ELEMENTS OF NATURE

> Let us keep our hearts young and our eyes open
> that nothing worth our while shall escape us.
> – Victor Cherbuliez –

I'm sitting on a bench in a covered pavilion at the Japanese Garden in Cheekwood, our local botanical gardens. Silently I settle into my surroundings: gentle rolling hills, the windswept look of black pines with limbs pointing up to the always changing cloudscape, a cherry tree that has yet to bloom, a line of bamboo bowing in the breeze, and gray boulders outlining a carpet of smaller stones raked in curved, flowing patterns. With my eye, I follow the undulating parallel lines in the stones and think about how we humans interact with and build from nature. It's most often nature that evokes wonder in me, but the human-made world can do the same from raked stones to a preschooler's spirals of bright crayon to the masterpieces of famous painters, sculptors, composers, and poets; from footprints in wet sand to handprints in concrete; from a skyscraper to a thatched hut. The beauty that people create from the elements of nature invites me to linger and fills me with wonder. And wonder, I believe, is a kind of gratitude.

6. Sun Puddles

It's a cold winter day, and I'm sitting in the warmest place in our house: a chair next to a south window where the sun is shining in. The warmth feels like a sun hug. Djimma, our cat, seeks out patches of sun too. Wherever she finds puddles of sun, she takes full advantage and dozes in the bright warmth. Of course, sun puddles dim and cool if clouds roll in.

Even if there are no clouds, sun puddles are shape shifters, moving across the floor as the sun treks across the sky and changes shape, now a long rectangle, now a square or a rhombus or a bisected triangle. Sun puddles are the closest companions of shadows. The two interplay, defining each other in fascinating designs. Pause a moment today to notice the friendship of shadows and sun puddles.

7 BENEATH OUR FEET

> Black are my steps on silver sod;
> Thick blows my frosty breath abroad;
> And tree and house, and hill and lake,
> Are frosted like a wedding cake.
> – Robert Louis Stevenson –

One of my delights in teaching preschoolers for several years was watching children learn the way they naturally and joyfully do at that age: hands-on and using all their senses. Sometimes I would bring flat items of different textures to class so they could walk across them with bare feet. Bubble wrap, corrugated cardboard, linoleum tiles, carpet samples, we lined them up and walked across, tiptoed across, hopped across, stomped across. We examined and described each texture and enjoyed the whole experience. As you walk today, now and then pause for a minute to focus on how the ground or floor feels beneath your feet.

8. DISCOVERY

A few minutes ago, I was digging around in the back of a small-tool drawer, looking for a tack just the right size to hang a picture. In addition to finding a tack, I also discovered three strands of shiny Mardi Gras beads that a friend gave us years ago. One strand was magenta, one was silver, and one was purple. Not knowing quite what to do with them, I left them in the drawer, but not before lingering with them, feeling the roundness of the beads, watching the glint of light on them, enjoying the way the colors twined in their tangle, listening to the rattle as I dropped them back into their resting place, where I will no doubt someday discover them again.

Reach into a drawer or closet shelf, and see what's been pushed to the back. Linger with it for a moment before moving on.

9. HORIZONS

My oldest grandson once asked why the section of town I live in is called Green Hills. "Because we're in the hills," I said, waving my hand southward. "You can see most of the hills in that direction." But that wasn't exactly true. The hills are in that direction, but it was summertime, and it was impossible to see anything past the full trees. Now it's winter, the trees are bare, and we can see all the way to the horizon, the green hills. So I showed him again. "There they are. Those are the green hills."

I grew up in the flat plains of West Texas, where the sky is wide, the trees are few, and the line where earth meets the heavens is clearly visible. How far can you see? Where's your horizon?

10. SOCKS

One of the pleasures of winter, for me, is warm socks, especially when they come straight from the dryer. And I confess that I sometimes skate across the hardwood floors in my socks, although I did it more often when I was younger. Sock skating probably speeds up the retiring of socks that surprise me with a cold spot because of a hole in the toe or heel. The next time you pull on socks—or slippers if you're not a sock person—spend a minute noticing them and being grateful for this small gift of softness and warmth.

11. A WHISPERY WHOOSH

In the dew of little things
the heart finds its
morning and is refreshed.
– Kahlil Gibran –

Cold weather has always been accompanied by the hum and faint whispery whoosh of the heater turning on, bringing with it a dusty smell with a burnt edge. When I notice it, I like to linger with it. The sound is calming. The smell is comforting. It's a gentle blanket of all's-well.

12. THE FEEL OF ROUND

I'm cupping a small red potato in my hands. I'll be eating it with other roasted vegetables for dinner tonight. But right now, I'm lingering with it for a moment. It's cold, having just come out of the refrigerator, and it's smooth except for the faint, rough dips where the eyes are. It has no smell. And when I roll it between my palms, I can imagine that it's a ball of play dough or silly putty. But I'm glad it's not. Because this ball is tasty—or will be once I roast it and serve it with a little salt and butter.

At home or in the supermarket, cup a roundish fruit or vegetable in both hands—an orange or lemon, a potato or onion or turnip. Or maybe something smaller like a berry or a grape. Feel its weight, its shape, its texture. Smell it. Maybe even taste it.

13. A WINTER MOON

I saw Eternity the other night
Like a great ring of pure and endless light,

All calm, as it was bright.
– Henry Vaughan –

We had a full moon last week, and I lingered with it, watching it climb the sky. Something about the round glow of a full moon is warmly satisfying to me. A full moon makes me feel full too. Perhaps it's simply the act of pausing to notice nature that gives me a sense of wholeness. "Wholeness is our deepest need," we sang in a hymn at church last Sunday. Maybe that's why the full moon warms me. It's a symbol of wholeness.

14. NATURAL HEARTS

Crossing a bare common,
in snow puddles,
at twilight,
under a clouded sky . . .
I have enjoyed a perfect exhilaration.
– Ralph Waldo Emerson –

In my yard, there's a vine with heart-shaped leaves that grows wild and climbs whatever it can reach. Its leaves stay on the vine all through the winter. It's not ivy, which also has vaguely heart-shaped leaves and grows in our front garden. This is a different vine. It climbs high into the trees if it's not cut back. A few winters ago, I looked out my bedroom window and saw that this vine was not only hanging high in a tree but that it had formed itself into a circle, a wreath of hearts that I hadn't noticed when the tree was in leaf. Now that the tree's leaves had fallen, there it was, as if the birds had hung it to decorate the yard. Since then, I've looked for hearts formed naturally by leaves, petals, sun and shadow, wood, or anything surprising. While you're noticing hearts today, see if you can spy any that have formed naturally.

15. WET CLOTHES

My four-year-old grandson recently helped me transfer clothes from the washer to the dryer. As I pulled them out of the washer, a few at a time, and handed them to him, we shivered and said, "Ooh! Wet!" We both laughed at how the damp clothes felt in our hands. Then, of course, about an hour later, we took them out of the dryer, soft and warm and dry—or for denims and canvas work pants, not soft at all. But warm. And dry. Not only does my grandson help me with the laundry, but he also helps me remember to linger.

16. IMPERFECTIONS

I recently read artist Makoto Fujimura's book *Art and Faith*. Throughout, he refers to kintsugi, which he defines as "the ancient Japanese art form of repairing broken tea ware by reassembling ceramic pieces." He writes that kintsugi "creates anew the valuable pottery, which now becomes more beautiful and more valuable than the original, unbroken vessel."

I thought of my house, which was built in 1935. It's old and well-lived-in. There are lots of cracks and creaks and repaired places. Maybe no guest would notice the repairs in the plaster ceiling of the living room or the patched walls or the filled-in scratches on the hardwood floors. But I'm now eyeing them, lingering with them, appreciating them as part of a house's aging process. I'm viewing repairs as a way of creating anew a house more beautiful and more valuable. By the way, if you linger with the idea of kintsugi, you may even start applying it to yourself.

17. PAGES

David Whyte's *River Flow*, Margaret Renkl's *Late Migrations*, Mary Oliver's *A Poetry Handbook*—these are the books currently on my nightstand. Real hold-them-in-your-hand-and-turn-the-paper-pages books. I know that more and more reading is done from screens these days, and I read on screens as well, but there's something much more satisfying to me about the act of reading a real paper-paged book. Friends sometimes ask what movies, TV shows, or series I watch. The answer is very few. I prefer the slow act of reading, both with fiction and nonfiction. Reading doesn't rush me through in increments of screen minutes. Instead, it provides a slower, more thoughtful, more thorough dive into whatever world the book or magazine presents. I can thumb through a book at my own pace. I can pause, savor, linger, and think. And it's a sensory experience. I can ruffle the pages and smooth my hand over the texture, slick and crisp or old and soft. I can smell a book. And that's a joy.

Pause to notice the sensory experience of a book or magazine.

18. BERRIES

> Distant ancient light
> Kisses red winter berries,
> Timeless touches time.
> – kh –

I lingered in our side yard for a moment today, struck by how the angle of winter sunlight brightens the nandina berries, making them stand out red orange against the green foliage of the bush. I was struck by how light from our ancient sun is plumping up a bunch of berries in this present moment. Today. Before my eyes. The timeless is touching time.

19. SEEDS

Seeds in their seasons,
slowly, surely, steadily
enfold life
calmly waiting
through dark days
and chill frost,
holding life
snug and secure
for the time when they will
crack open to light
and life
and wonder.
– kh –

I've learned to linger with seeds, those in the garden in pods, like the basil on my back deck still clinging to their dried stems, and those not yet in the garden, like the dried beans and peas I occasionally use for soups and chili. But my lingering goes beyond seeds for gardening and eating. Seeds are part of a practice I learned at the Art & Soul studio. There we have a variety of random material to inspire us to play and create—rocks, driftwood, ribbons, shells, and baskets of seeds. I find it calming to stir dried beans and seeds with my fingers, to scoop a handful out of a basket, to pour them back in quickly or slowly. It's amazing how still I can become by simply focusing on feeling their shapes, listening to them shower back down, watching them tumble through my fingers. Seeds are tiny miracles.

20. STEAM

After my shower today, I drew a flower in the steam on my bathroom mirror. When you were a child, did you ever breathe on a cold window to steam it up and then draw in the steam? I remember doing this on car windows. I also remember that it was an unapproved activity, because it left smudges on the window that had to be cleaned off. Sometimes no one was around to witness the secret writing in steam, but telltale smudges revealed the act. Now it's usually my bathroom mirror that I notice steamed up after a hot shower. When I linger with it, I smile. A secret smile. A mischievous smile. Drawing on it still feels subversive. But then, I'm the one who has to clean it up, so why not?

21. COLORS

In Leo Lionni's book *Frederick*, a family of mice spends the last weeks of summer busily gathering food for the cold winter months. Everyone scampers here and there doing their part—everyone but Frederick, who sits in the sun gazing dreamily. When cold weather comes, the mice hole up in their underground burrow and eat the food they've stored. But one day, the last bit of food is gone, and it's not yet spring. That's when Frederick shares what he gathered: colors. Frederick encourages the mice with memories of the colors of warmer months, memories that sustain them until warmer weather arrives.

That's what we were doing back in those days of childhood, you and I, as we lay in the grass or slowly swayed in a swing or tossed a stone into water to watch the ripples or listened to birds call from tree to tree. We were lingering, gathering colors and shapes and sounds and smells and textures and flavors that, even now, we can close our eyes and see and hear and smell. We were gathering childlike joy for this season of our lives. We were gathering wonder.

22. SQUIRRELS

Squirrels leap lightly,
startling snow-laden branches,
showering snow below.
– kh –

Like many of my neighbors, I have a love/hate relationship with squirrels. They've been venturing out on cold days to snoop around my deck, snatching up sunflower seeds that fall from the squirrel-proof bird feeder. They can be pesky pests. But they can also be fascinating creatures with their watchful, dark eyes and lithe bodies standing erect and alert, or hunkering low to sniff out food, or digging where they buried seeds or nuts last autumn, or stretching their bushed-out tails over their heads like an umbrella to protect them from rain. I enjoy pausing to watch squirrels chase each other around a tree trunk, circling higher and higher until they reach the upper branches, where they use the longest limb as a bridge that ends in thin air. But that's no problem. They leap across the gap into the next tree and continue the race.

23. A HINT OF SPRING

Overnight, it seems,
bushes and shrubs –
the mahonia, the sweetspire,
the rhododendron –
have burst into full blossom
outsmarting old winter.
Too early, I whisper,
too early.
They shiver, these blossoms,
these bright,
white
blooms
of snow.
– kh –

Sometimes spring sashays in for a few days in winter in spite of what the calendar says. The gardeners around here advise us not to plant anything until at least April 15. But when that hint of spring dances in, it's hard to hold back.

24. NEIGHBORS

> Square of red and gold,
> neighbor window in the night,
> warms me that you're home.
> – kh –

There's something comforting about a light in a window on a dark, cold winter day. I once drove through a small town in Ohio, where it seemed there was a candle in every window of every house, and it felt so cheery. Light from a window, even if it comes from a candle, feels like a welcome, as if it's saying, "We're home, and you are welcome here." In my writer's imagination, I think of sons and daughters who have been away for a while and are returning home, looking to see if a light was left on for them and finding a light in every window. During the winter holidays, I put candles in my windows to say the same.

Look for windows filled with light. Linger a moment with the joy and welcome they offer.

25. WINTER BIRDS

Wren song, cheery clear,
rings through the chill winter sky,
praise to life out on a limb.
– kh –

Listen for the winter birds, those hardy creatures who sing into the cold.

26. YOUR OWN FACE

When I was about five years old, my aunt showed me how to draw a profile of a lady. I've been drawing and painting faces ever since. Faces fascinate me, especially eyes, so I pay attention to proportions. A face from chin to top of the forehead is the length of that person's hand. Try it. Put the heel of your hand at your chin and reach up. The tip of your middle finger is at about the top of your forehead. Your eyes are right above the halfway mark on your face. The tip of your nose is about halfway between your eyes and chin, and your mouth is about halfway between the tip of your nose and your chin. And here's another measurement that fascinates me: The space between your eyes is the width of one of your eyes. When I watch a news anchor on TV, I automatically scan their face to confirm that it's true. And it always is.

27. WATCH FOR SURPRISES

I thought it was a cardinal,
that flash of red
through snowy branches.
But it was so still,
not the here-and-gone
flitting of wings.
Then a gust of wind
shook the tree
and it soared free
into the chilled sky:
a red balloon.

– kh –

28. WINTER STORM

The sled and traveller stopped, the courier's feet
Delayed, all friends shut out, the housemates sit
Around the radiant fireplace, enclosed
In a tumultuous privacy of storm.
– Ralph Waldo Emerson –

Sometimes our electricity goes out in a storm,
usually an ice storm, darkening the day and forcing
us to slow down and pause and look at our world in
a smaller circle than before. We see from a different
perspective, one that's dim during the day and, at

night, flickers by candlelight or shrinks to the width of the beam of a flashlight. For warmth, the cat burrows under the quilt on the top bunk in "the boys' room," the boys having grown up and left home quite some time ago. I wrap up in a quilt by the fireplace. Emerson was right. It's a tumultuous privacy.

29. A MOMENT OF PEACE

Here's an old blessing I linger with when I need a moment of peace.

Deep peace of the running wave to you.
Deep peace of the flowing air to you.
Deep peace of the quiet earth to you.
Deep peace of the shining stars to you.
– based on the writings of poet William Sharp –

MARCH

1. A GLAD BEGINNING

"Dear March—come in! How glad I am!"
– Emily Dickinson –

Quietly comes
the dance of dawn,
shy glance of light,
spreading easy as a smile
at the pleasure of giving

its first faint glow,
a warm invitation
to shake off shadows
Sweet breath of beginning,
springtime of hours,
tints the world tender with
touches of azure,
washes of whisper green,
thin lines of lemon gold,
and a blush
that grows bolder,
sharpens the sky,
and stretches
into the full light
of day.
– kh –

2. A WORLD ASTIR

…Winter still is in the air,
And the earth troubled, and the branches bare,
Yet down the fields to-day I saw her pass—
The spring—her feet went shining through the grass…
she has whispered to the crocus leaves…
She would not stay, her season is not yet,
But she has reawakened, and has set
The sap of all the world astir…
– John Drinkwater –

There comes a day between winter and spring when the garden seems to prick up its ears and lift its nose (it would if it were a rabbit) and sense the approach of warmer weather. Just an inkling, a tickle, a prickle, a knowing that glances east, scans the west, eyes the north and south. The weather is changing.

Listen for spring's whisper, linger with it, and breathe deeply of the quiet hope of a world astir.

3. ROCKS

My youngest grandson visited today and brought me a gift that he held in one fist: a rock about an inch and a half long. It's not anything spectacular, just a common rock, brown mottled with white, lumpy and pitted. Even so, it's a treasure. It now resides on the windowsill above my kitchen sink with a variety of other treasures.

Rocks and pebbles are quietly faithful, usually easy to find, and so common that we step on or over them, passing them by without noticing how varied they are. But they're just right for lingering with. Pick one up. Feel its texture. Notice its color. Maybe pocket it. Maybe keep it on your kitchen windowsill.

4. SHOES

New shoes automatically make you run faster, or so my preschool grandson insists. He also insists on proving it. He knows how to appreciate his shoes.

Appreciate is an interesting word. It comes from a Latin word that means price. When something appreciates—like hopefully your house or funds you've invested toward retirement—its price or value increases. So, appreciating something or someone not only recognizes their value but also increases their value.

Linger with your shoes as you put them on, or focus for a moment on the ones you're wearing. Wiggle your toes. Appreciate them. See if they make you run faster.

5. NATURE'S TUG OF WAR

Silver rain turns to
crystal ice, gray clouds sprinkle
glittersnow. Magic.
– kh –

This is a time when it seems nature can't make up her mind. One day, spring whispers. The next day, Winter says, "Not yet." They have a tug of war for a while. But Spring wins in the end, and we know she will.

6. LOOKING OR SEEING?

Last Sunday, partway through our church service, I noticed a soft, horizontal, rectangular shadow that crosses the upper part of the pastel yellow wall at the front of the sanctuary. The wall is so familiar that I hadn't really seen what was always there: a shadow cast by an exposed beam crossing the space just beneath the apex of the ceiling high above the balcony, the space that holds and amplifies the voices of the choir, the reading of the liturgy, and the prayers of the people. It made me wonder what else I've missed when I've looked without seeing.

Lingering is a way of pulling our attention into the present moment, a way of giving ourselves the opportunity to not only look but also see.

7. WATER

This afternoon, we had a downpour that overflowed the gutter above the windows by my desk, turning the view into a waterfall. The rain has stopped now, but it left droplets glittering like diamonds on the window screens. Water in any form is endlessly interesting. Ripples in a pond can be mesmerizing.

Sea waves frothing and churning, ebbing and surging can be both calming and stirring at the same time.

But that's just the visual effect. Water offers us texture, too—the warm, floaty feel of a bath; the cleansing hot spray of a shower; the chilly splash into a pool. Or as Helen Keller described it, "the wonderful cool something that was flowing over my hand." And there's nothing like the coolness of a drink of pure water when I'm thirsty.

Then there are the sounds water makes. It sprays, swishes, swashes, dribbles, bubbles, gurgles, and splashes. It splatters, slooshes and sloshes, pitter-pats, drip-drops, and sizzles in a hot pan. Water is part of nature's music and magic. Notice water today in puddles or drips or sprays or ripples. Cup it in your hands, sip it, let it run through your fingers. Let yourself linger with the gift of water.

8. BRIDGES

A storm gust cracked
a frail, leafless branch,
a large twig, really,
thin and gray and slightly curved.
It sailed to the ground,
landed lightly on three tips
like tiny limbs, fingers and toes.
They touched down,
kept the backbone from breaking,

> held the arched spine off the ground,
> a tiny bridge for ants to cross.
> On second thought,
> not frail at all.
> – kh –

To me, there's something fascinating about bridges. I think part of my fascination comes from being inspired by the connections they make, their here-to-thereness. Another part of my fascination is with the beauty and variety of bridges: stone bridges with arches, train bridges with trestles, suspension bridges, swinging bridges, rope bridges. Then there are bridges formed by nature from large rock formations to tiny bridges mostly unnoticed but crossed by ants. Once I saw an inchworm cross a gap between deck boards. For a moment, she was her own bridge.

Look for a bridge, large or small, and pause for a moment to notice it. A bridge makes a way. It's an invitation to journey on and discover. Or to journey back and return.

9. AJAR

The catch on one of my kitchen cabinets broke this week, so the cabinet stands ajar. The way my mind works, once I notice something, I begin seeing it everywhere. I never noticed until now how many things are ajar around here: the closet door in my bedroom, which has never closed properly; the mailbox, hard to shut tight; a notebook, ready for me to write in; the lid on a jar candle, which I never closed all the way; a friend's handmade greeting card that I keep on display; the drawer of a hutch; a box of toy blocks. They all stand partially open, expectant, waiting for some kind of closure.

10. THE WORLD WAKING UP

To me the meanest flower that blows can give
Thoughts that do often lie too deep for tears.
– William Wordsworth –

Gardens did not interest me much when I was a child in Texas. My parents grew easy and persistent plants like four o'clocks, cannas, and honeysuckle. I was more interested in digging for land snails or searching for horned toads. But as I've grown older and moved to a greener state, I've fallen in love with gardens. And I've discovered that not all flowers bloom at the same time. Now that's not a revelation for garden lovers, but I'd had the simplistic idea that all flowers bloomed in the spring. I learned that here, even with snow on the ground, crocuses emerge first with their purple petals and splash of yellow in the center. Daffodils bloom in February, which seems too soon, but they're the real sign that warmer weather is on its way. From there, it seems that the rest of the garden wakes up for good. What's blooming right now where you live? What's waking up?

11. SILENCE

> . . . Let thy west wind sleep on
> The lake; speak silence with thy glimmering eyes,
> And wash the dusk with silver. . . .
> – William Blake –

So much of nature speaks in silence, and it's most often when we're silent that we hear it. Ours is a noisy world. Find time to settle into silence and linger there for a moment, listening to nature.

12. FOG

> A soft wash of fog
> fades the far branches,
> cushions the green-gold of leaves,
> gentles the morning,
> a sheer curtain drawn across the dawn,
> easing the weary world into wakefulness,
> whispering the day into attentiveness,
> soothing and settling dreams
> into lingering in a drowsy world half awake,
> half asleep.

I know what's out there in the cotton mist. I've seen the crisp beauty,

and the obvious obstacles.
But for now, they are blanketed,
blurred into shapes with no sharp edges,
the way that each day lived forward
softens and blurs the past
and gazes toward the haze of what's to come.
– kh –

13. HOLES

I've found a hole in our front yard. I linger and eye it. Probably it was made by chipmunks. Or moles. The possibility of a snake crosses my mind. But I think it's too large for a snake . . . unless . . . no, I'll be optimistic and go with chipmunk, although that's not good news for the garden. Back indoors, I punch holes in a stack of papers, meeting minutes to place in the business folder at the Art & Soul Nashville studio where I'm the secretary on the board. Recently I even incorporated hole-punched paper into artwork. So punching holes is part of my job (just like digging holes is part of the chipmunk's job, unfortunately).

There are holes everywhere: in donuts and bagels, as a cat door, in my ear for earrings. Empty space to go through or just to look at. To lead somewhere or nowhere.

14. WATCHING A PINPOINT

A red edged pinpoint of white light
glides across the night sky,
a jet with an
urgent whispering growl
surging through,
pushing past
with promise,
leaving what was
to encounter what will be,
riding rivers of air,
connecting the points of life,
beginning of adventure
—or the end—
carrying hopes and disappointments,
dreads and dreams
in suspended state.
How many people
at any given time
are suspended between
above and below
in a thousand places an hour,
everywhere
yet nowhere,
with all things possible.
How many below
hear the urgent surge,

watch the pinpoint glide past overhead
and wish we, too, were up there,
suspended,
going somewhere.
–kh –

15. WIND

Wild and beckoning sky,
winged wind,
cloud-feathered,
earth's rising mist,
our drifting breath,
caught and curled and gathered
and breathed back to us in breeze,
our cries and laughter
sung back to us
in sparkling sleet
and pounding rain,
returned
so we can laugh

and love
and sweat
and live.
– kh –

Pay deep attention to the stirring of wind and
weather.

16. LINGERING WITH TEARS

Today,
I cannot pray.
No matter.
I hold her birdbone hand,
hold the heart-space,
breathe the depths
her failing lungs cannot access.
Today,
I am the prayer.
– kh –

Sometimes pain, physical or emotional, forces me
to linger when I'd rather turn my attention to
something brighter and lighter and cheerier. The
strange thing is, pain has a way of sharpening and
focusing my attention on what's right in front of me,
and I find myself lingering with the angle of a shadow,
the curve of a cup, the sharpness of a spice in my tea.
Pain has a way of opening up space for deep emotions
and vulnerability. I feel my throat tighten, my skin

prickle, tears well and flow, all part of the rich human experience. It's my turn to feel it, to linger with it, and that's okay. Tears are healthy, and lingering with them is healthy too.

17. FLAVORS

Browsing the food section of a recent catalogue from Vermont Country Store, I became intrigued by the descriptions of food. A hint of chocolate and raspberry. Round and robust. A crispy finish. Burst of tangy flavor. Subtle tang. Rich, earthy nuttiness. Slightly peppery at first bite. Bursting with the flavor of vibrant spring vegetables and bright herbs. Succulent. Delicately sweet. Intense flavor, sweet, yet slightly tart. Incredibly fruity. Rich, sweet flavor. Bursting with fresh-from-the-garden taste. Mellow tanginess and buttery flavor. (Okay, my mouth is watering now.) Some of these descriptions remind me of labels on specialty coffee. Or wine. And, really, just the name of a food can sometimes evoke the flavor. Pumpkin-spice, walnuts and apples, brown sugar cinnamon. Lemon. Maple. Honey. Blueberry, Raspberry, Strawberry. Chocolate.

I've enjoyed slowing down a bit, lingering over a meal, savoring what I eat—and wondering how I would describe the flavor.

18. PILLOW

I like lots of pillows on my bed—one for my head, one for my arms to hold, one to lean back against, and three for decoration after I make the bed. I considered getting a new pillow when my husband got one, but I know how to plump this old one just right to cradle my head. It's not hard for me to linger with a pillow and be grateful.

19. THE VIEW FROM THROUGH

As I tipped up the clear glass and finished the water in it, I noticed through the bottom a distorted view of the window I was facing and the trees beyond. The effect was almost kaleidoscopic. The dividers between the window panes were wavy. The trees beyond melted into a splash of color in lines that radiated starburst-like from the center. The next time you take a drink of clear liquid from a clear glass, linger a moment with what you can see through the bottom of it. Notice the way it distorts what's beyond, maybe the way it refracts the light, making it split into rainbows. At the least, you'll get a different perspective on the world.

20. WALLS

My house has a variety of textures on the walls: slick, shiny tile in one bathroom; white-painted wood paneling in another; rough plaster in the bedrooms; brick outside with some bumpy vinyl siding. At Art & Soul studio, many of the walls are paneled with Homosote fiber board so that we can tack up paintings, drawings, and collages we're working on. Slow down for a moment and run your hand across a wall or two as you pass. Let your fingertips give you information. If you can linger longer, get a piece of paper and a pencil or crayon. Place the paper on the wall and rub over it to get a visual of the texture. Change walls (and textures) and rub over it again. Enjoy.

21. AT THE SPRING

The year's at the spring,
And day's at the morn;
Morning's at seven;
The hill-side's dew-pearled;
The lark's on the wing;
The snail's on the thorn;
God's in His heaven –
All's right with the world!
– Robert Browning –

Linger with today's weather. Breathe it in. Breathe it out. Feel nature's majesty around you.

22. A WINDOW INTO SPRING

> Nature is painting for us,
> day after day,
> pictures of infinite beauty.
> – John Ruskin –

Linger at the window you chose to use as a frame (see January 19). How has the scene changed from winter? As a reminder: If your view is a nature scene, let it be a sacred space, a small revelation of nature. If your view is a building or other structure, let it be a small tribute to shapes, textures, and shadows. Either way, it's a unique view just for you.

23. THE GIANT BOX

My father is color-blind. So are both of my sons. They're all red-green deficient. That means they have a hard time seeing red berries or red blooms on a green tree. And I learned not to buy red balls for my sons, because red balls easily get lost in green grass. Still, each of my sons is quite good at art and design. It's just that they work in black and white. When my older son took art classes, his teacher taught him to work with hues and values, dark/light contrast. I can only imagine what that must be like, because I love colors. All colors. When I was in elementary school, I loved the giant box of crayons. I loved their names: cornflower blue, magenta, midnight blue, spring green, forest green, mahogany, burnt orange, dandelion, robin's egg blue. There are so many more tints and shades. I want to try them all. But that may take a while. They don't all fit in a giant box.

Linger with a color you like and let it cheer you.

24. GRASS

One of my favorite books when I was young was *Nibble, Nibble,* a book of poems by Margaret Wise Brown. The first section, "Deep In The Green Stemmed World," contains poems about the busy world hidden in the grass at our feet. She paints a word picture of a "long stemmed world" where bugs "buzz themselves to sleep." Pause a moment with this long-stemmed world. Pluck a blade or two of grass, even if it's dried or growing out of a crack in a sidewalk. Twirl it between your fingers. Clutch it in your palm. Sniff it. Or bend down and run your hand over a patch of grass. Linger with it for a moment.

25. PUDDLES

The sun loses nothing by shining into a puddle.
                        – a 14th century proverb –

I knew it was going to happen. On a walk through Cheekwood Botanical Gardens, I spied a large puddle ahead on the sidewalk. A mother and her two young sons were on the other side of the puddle heading my direction. They hadn't yet reached the puddle, but when they did, the two delighted boys jumped right in before their mom could say a word. Not long after that, on a rainy Sunday, I spied a puddle on the sidewalk on the way to my car after church. We'd had some baptisms that morning, a sacred rite with a font of water. When I got to the puddle, I decided that it, too, was sacred. I lingered a moment. Then I jumped in. With both feet.

26. MORNING SOUNDS

Dawn whispers morning,
hums the day before breaking
into full song.
– kh –

I enjoy sleeping with windows open when the weather allows. Fresh air drifts in, a breeze stirs the leaves in a shushing sound, and birds sing me awake. Listen for morning sounds as they come to you from indoors or out. If you can, linger with them for a moment before you start your day.

27. IN EVERY FAIR FACE

Never lose an opportunity of seeing anything that is
beautiful
for beauty is God's handwriting—a wayside
sacrament.
Welcome it in every fair face, in every fair sky, in
every fair flower,
and thank God for it as a cup of blessing.
– Ralph Waldo Emerson –

In my dictionary, the first meaning of the word *fair*
is *pleasing to the eye; beautiful*. The variety of faces
in this world is amazing, and, truly, every face holds
a quality that is uniquely fascinating and beautiful.
Pay attention to faces, to their shape, their length,
their width, the slope of a nose, the arc of eyebrows,
the shape of eyes and mouth. "Thank God for it as a
cup of blessing."

28. WAYS OF WALKING

"To find the universal elements enough; to find the air
and the water exhilarating; to be refreshed by a morning
walk or an evening saunter . . . to be thrilled by the stars
at night; to be elated over a bird's nest or a wildflower in
spring—these are some of the rewards of the simple life."
– John Burroughs –

When I was writing novels, I often searched for specific words that would describe the way characters walked. Did they saunter, sashay, stomp, trudge, or weave? Did they creep, shuffle, stride, or plod? John Burroughs hints that he is refreshed by a morning walk. Or an evening saunter. Without judging, simply notice the way you walk. How would you describe it?

29. DANCING IN A SUNBEAM

One of the fascinations of childhood—and one that continues to fascinate me—is the way dust motes show up when sunlight shines through a window at just the right angle. As I was making waffles today, a bit of the baking powder that I added to the flour drifted up into a sunbeam and added to the slow dance of the dust motes in the beam of light. I bent my head to get a better look and linger for a couple of seconds before I finished making the waffles. Of course, dust motes are present all the time, dancing all around us in the air. They're simply unnoticed until the sun shines its spotlight on them and I decide to linger.

30. CONFESSION

I have to confess: I just killed a large roach with Rilke's *Book of Hours*. I did linger with it a moment— the roach, not the book. I think I was in shock, because the roach was on the shade of my bedside lamp. Plus, I hadn't seen a roach in a long time, and it's been ages since I saw one this big. It was as long as my pointer finger and shiny rust-red with delicate wings folded against its back. I was a bit fascinated by its two antennae, which were as long as half its body and thread-thin, waving gently as if testing the vibes. Then it jump-flew to the side of my nightstand, and I jump-flew into action. I grabbed the closest thing at hand—Rilke—and hit the roach. Pretty hard. It seemed rather sacrilegious to use the Book of Hours for that purpose. Sorry, Rilke. It's now back on the nightstand—the book, not the roach. The roach is no more. There are obviously some things I don't want to linger with too long.

31. SAVORING

> O for a beaker full of the warm South.
> – John Keats –

In his poem "Ode to a Nightingale," John Keats yearns for a vintage that tastes "of Flora and the country green." He seems to be tasting a memory. He pines for a beaker of warm South. For me, the warm South is the Southwest, and the Southwest is Texas where I grew up. So the beaker full of warm South is a pitcher of peppery barbecue sauce, ready to pour on a slice of smoked beef brisket. "O for a beaker full of the warm South." I can almost taste it now. Anyone who has eaten Texas barbecue sauce knows it's worth slowing down and savoring.

What's your favorite beaker full of? What memory do you taste in it?

SPRING

APRIL

1. SPRING SKY

> The blue sky is the temple's arch,
> Its transept earth and air,
> The music of its starry march
> The chorus of a prayer.
> – John Greenleaf Whittier –

The sky is the cathedral of nature. Lingering with it is a kind of prayer.

2. WINGS OF SPRING

> My heart in hiding
> Stirred for a bird.
> – Gerard Manley Hopkins –

Warm-weather birds are returning and seem quite happy to be back. Some mornings I look out my window to see my yard full of robins busily pecking around in the grass. That must mean bugs and worms are emerging as well. And this year, I'm hearing a mockingbird with his ever-changing song. I've seen him a few times in a flash of white as he flies, and I hope he stays around. One of my joys is lingering with these birds, and the mockingbird adds to the joyful chorus.

3. YOUR TREE

> Though we travel the world over
> to find the beautiful,
> we must carry it with us
> or we find it not.
> – Ralph Waldo Emerson –

What's happening with the tree you chose to follow through the seasons (see January 6)? How is it changing? Or maybe the tree's not changing but its surroundings are.

4. LANDSCAPE

> Geography and landscape shape us.
> Weather blows in through our souls.
> – Beth Kephart –

Driving home from my younger son's house, I crest a hill, and the skyline of downtown Nashville comes into view with its distinctive Batman building (that's what we call it, because each side of its roof rises to a point like Batman's hood). It's easy for me to drive across town without thinking even once about its geography. Houses and neighborhoods, buildings and trees tend to obscure the land and distract my attention from the terrain. But if I pay attention as I drive, I begin to be aware of hills and valleys, streams and rivers. I begin to notice the landscape of this place on the globe where I live. I begin to appreciate the geography of my location.

Take a minute now and then to notice your landscape.

5. REDISCOVER MAGIC

The world is full of magic things,
patiently waiting for our senses to grow sharper.
– W.B. Yeats –

A budding tulip, a bird calling to its mate, the pink clouds of sunset, the first star of evening—it only takes a moment to sharpen our senses to this everyday magic, to pause and actually taste our food, smell the morning air, feel the breeze, hear birdsong, and see the beauty in the world around us. To rediscover the magic things.

6. A VOICE

My youngest grandson is working on learning the sounds that different letters make. We're currently working on the consonants that are pronounced the same except for the fact that one is voiced and one is not. Like g and k. Or f and v. Or b and p. I place his hand on my throat and then on his throat to feel how a voiced consonant vibrates our voice box and an unvoiced one doesn't. Linger with your voice for a minute, gently pressing your hand to your throat, feeling the vibrations as you sing along to music or simply speak.

7. APRIL FLOWERS

Spring night,
cherry-
blossom dawn.
– Matsuo Basho –

A few years ago, I went to Japan to visit my older son and his family, who live there. I knew the cherry trees blossomed around that time of year, but their blooming depends on the weather, so no one can predict exactly when it will be. Fortunately for me, it happened the week I arrived. We picnicked alongside other families in a park full of cherry trees—sakura—rich with pink blooms. We strolled paths lined with cherry blossoms and delighted in the delicate breeze-blown petals that drifted gently to the ground. It was a time to pause and wonder at the beauty and peace of spring. We have cherry trees here in Tennessee, too. And pear trees, peach trees, plums. They're so stunning that I think most of us just naturally pause to appreciate such a gift.

8. WINDOWS

When I was in school as a student, and later as a teacher, I would look out the windows of the classroom and wonder what other people were doing while I was in school. A whole world was passing by, people with stories and jobs, places to go and things to do. Even now, one of the first things I look for in a house is windows. Bay windows, compass windows, arched windows, sidelights, picture windows, rose windows, oriels, stained glass, mullioned . . . I love windows. I want windows. I need windows. They are my view to the world. They are a perfect place to linger.

9. A PALM FULL

The blueberries at the supermarket this week were huge—almost the diameter of a quarter. I had heard that larger berries were the sweetest, so I bought some. This morning I opened the container, wondering how many huge berries would equal the number of small berries that I usually put in my oatmeal. Then I realized that the actual number didn't matter. I usually measure out a palm full of berries, which is 1/2 cup, one serving. A palm full is a palm full whether the berries are large or small. So I scooped up a palm full of huge, blue-black berries and washed them, feeling the water pouring over their plump, round bodies, noticing the way the morning light reflected in an arc around each berry. Then I settled them onto my oatmeal and took a bite. A berry split and spread over my tongue in a tart burst of flavor that held a touch of sweetness. What a treat, these big-bellied blueberries.

10. FROM A CHILD'S VIEW

When my preschool grandson was here last week, he hid small "treasures" around the house, most of them tiny, gold, plastic coins from a play pirate set. He didn't retrieve them before he went home, so I tried to locate them all as I cleaned up. But I'm still finding treasure in random places. I finally decided that maybe the best way to search for this treasure would be to get down on my knees at my grandson's level and take a look around. If I were four, where would I tuck a treasure?

One way of seeing our everyday surroundings from a new perspective is to lower ourselves. How does the world look when I'm on my knees? Or lying on my back on the floor. If you do yoga or other exercises, the next time you lie down, linger there for a moment and notice the world. Take a child's-eye view.

11. Drops of Water

> Little drops of water,
> Little grains of sand,
> Make the mighty ocean
> And the beauteous land.
>
> – Julia A. Carney –

Often after a rain, I go outdoors and wander around my garden taking pictures of raindrops. There's something elegant about water droplets on leaves and petals, the way they form beads and reflect the light. But I also find droplets when I water plants outside. I find them in the sink and bathtub, running down the walls of the shower, dripping from the faucet, and pooling on my skin before I dry off after bathing. Pause to appreciate a drop of water today.

12. Spring Leaves

Our neighbor, a young man, looked up into one of our elm trees and said he thought it was dead. But I knew it wasn't. Silhouetted against the sky, the branches had bumps on them, small nodes where buds were growing and about to emerge. Sure enough, within a week, the elm was in full leaf. I've seen these signs before on bare branches that are late to leaf out. Each spring, I watch the bush outside my kitchen window as it births its leaves. Small bumps swell and then open into tiny yellow-green curls of leaves that unfurl like small flags. Day by day they grow until they're large and bright green. They huddle together, casting dark green shadows on each other in the setting sun.

If, for a minute, you can step near a bush or tree where new leaves are emerging, gently pull a branch close and notice their shape and color. Witness their birth.

13. SIGNS OF THE SEASON

Set wide the window.
Let me drink the day.
– Edith Wharton –

At the moment, what's your favorite sign of the season? It can be a bit of nature or a flavor, a fragrance, or an inner sense, like anticipation or relief. Linger with it when you can. Tuck the thought of it into your soul and carry it with you.

14. Treetops

> The glassy peartree leaves and blooms, they brush
> The descending blue; that blue is all in a rush
> With richness.
> – Gerard Manley Hopkins –

Where recently the fingertips of bare winter branches touched the sky, leaves now reach up and out swayed by breezes, whipped by gusts, and on a still day, as steady as sentinels. The crowns of trees, especially that tip-top point where leaves meet sky, are one of my favorite sights in all the world. I don't know why. But when I'm outdoors, I often look up to the grand towering skylines of trees. Treetops inspire me and give me a hopeful feeling, an expansive sense of life and goodness above and beyond my reach but worth reaching for.

15. Borders

A surveyor marked our property line recently so that we could replace our old chain-link fence with a new, dark iron one. At intervals along the property line, he staked a short post with a red ribbon tied to it like a flag marking our border. Now I'm noticing borders everywhere: a stand of bamboo (called a canebrake around here), hedges, sidewalks, roads, streams. All of them form borders and have borders. Walls. The edges of rugs. Moldings around ceilings and floors and cabinets. Frames. Spaces around text in a book. Borders limit whatever they outline but seem to be unlimited in size and color and texture. I run my finger across the topstitching on my shirt (soft and bumpy), the spiral along my notebook (hard and twisty), the frame of my laptop screen (smooth and stiff). So many borders.

16. SAND AND DIRT

> To see a World in a Grain of Sand
> And a Heaven in a Wild Flower,
> Hold Infinity in the palm of your hand
> And Eternity in an hour.
> – William Blake –

At the Art & Soul Nashville studio, we have an enormous variety of materials to play with. One of those is sand. I've spent time with this sand, drawing lazy trails through it, scooping it up and letting it sift through my fingers, feeling its fine grain, hearing the soft shush as it spills back into itself, watching a mound form under my hands, seeing the dip of my handprint. It's a sensory, soothing practice. Even when I'm gardening, I hesitate to wear gloves. Feeling the dirt seems to be part of the process. Years ago, when I made pottery, the feel of the muddy slip and pliable clay connected me to the work. It's satisfying to run a finger over dirt, sand, or clay, to rub it between my fingers and linger a moment with the texture.

17. THE SCENT OF SPRING

In the 18th century, poet Alexander Pope wrote about "Isles of fragrance, lily-silver'd vales." The isle of fragrance that I think about is a field of hyacinths— pink, white, and purple—at Cheek-wood Botanical Gardens. It may be cliché to say the scent is heavenly, but . . . it is heavenly. Transporting. Nature's invitation to linger. Nature has so many invitations in spring. Blooms of all kinds. The rich smell of dirt. The fresh scent of approaching rain. The sharp green smell of newly mowed grass. It's worth reminding myself to linger when I step outdoors, to take a deep breath and catch the scent of spring.

18. FOLDS AND WRINKLES

To the left of my desk hangs a wall calendar of portraits of women reading. I'm awed by the skill of artists who create dimensional faces and figures on flat canvas. One thing that fascinates me is the way they paint fabrics, the folds and wrinkles, the light and dark, the line and texture. It makes me aware of the folds of my own clothes when I wear them, when I fold them, when I hang them in my closet or place them in a drawer. Sometimes I linger for a moment and run my hand across a shirt or pair of pants, feeling the texture with my fingertips. Our fingertips tell us so much.

Pause to look closely at a bit of fabric, maybe your shirt. Notice where it's darkest, where it's lightest, and how it feels under your fingertips.

19. LIGHT

> Is it so small a thing
> To have enjoyed the sun,
> To have lived light in the spring,
> To have loved, to have thought, to have done.
> – Matthew Arnold –

To me, Arnold's words "lived light" hold three meanings at once: live light, being unencumbered; live light, enjoying the sunshine of spring; live light, being a light ourselves. Live light!

20. TRIANGLES

When my mother made cheeseburgers every Sunday night, she would take a stack of square sliced cheese and cut the four corners off all the way through the stack to make octagons of cheese that fit better on the burgers. That left the cut-off corners, now stacks of triangles, for us kids to nibble on while waiting for supper. Triangles are a fun shape. I've noticed triangles in sections of sky peeking between clouds. The long leaves on my aloe plant crisscross, creating negative spaces shaped like triangles. My wine-red shamrocks are triangles that close their three triangular leaves into one folded triangle at night. Triangles are not as easy to find in my world as squares and circles, so I feel privileged when I spy one.

21. REFLECTIONS IN GLASS

This morning I lingered a moment to marvel at how my neighbor's side windows reflect the morning sky and trees. It reminded me of the time I saw trees reflected in the upper windows of Cheekwood mansion. The reflections were as clear as a painting and looked stunning next to the stone walls of the building. It stopped me in my own steps. I'm lucky to have a glass top on my kitchen table beside some large windows. The tabletop always gifts me with reflections of the outdoors.

When you see reflections in glass, especially reflections of nature, pause a minute to take in the view.

22. RANDOM OBJECTS

I do not understand;
I pause;
I examine.
– Michel de Montaigne –

In one of our kitchen drawers, toward the back, I just now found a cheap but fancy eight-inch sword with an ornate metal hilt in a black plastic sheath. (I feel I must note that while I keep coupons and transparent tape and a couple of sharpie markers in this drawer, it has also accumulated its share of junk. Thus the sword, which at first, I didn't recognize.) I pulled the sword out of the sheath and recalled that it's a souvenir letter opener that one of my sons bought somewhere we went. (Where, I don't remember.) Memoirist Beth Kephart says, "Every object signifies." So what does this sword letter opener signify? I would say it signifies my son's imagination and his attraction to beauty and adventure. It also signifies his growing up and leaving parts of that behind for me to find.

Open a random drawer—the notorious "junk drawer" works well—and take out an object that either draws you or repels you. Linger with it. Feel its shape and texture, note the color, note any sound it makes or any scent it has. What does that object

signify to you—or if not to you, to whom? Is it
important? Why is it in the drawer?

23. LINGER IN A RITUAL

It's almost time to make breakfast. I've made my
bed, washed my face, and dressed for the day. Now I
pause and stretch out and up while breathing deeply.
Ten times. I'm trying to make this a ritual. Ritual
sounds like a spiritual practice, but I don't necessarily
think of it that way. Getting ready for bed is a ritual.
Making breakfast is a ritual. Sitting down at my laptop
involves ritual. Folding clothes fresh from the dryer is
a ritual. Many practices at art class are rituals. When
I slow down, bring my mind into the present, and
make these activities sensory experiences, I feel and
appreciate the ritual experience they offer. And that
elevates these ordinary practices into the realm of the
spiritual.

Linger with a ritual today.

24. TO BE BORN

Nature always wears the colors of the spirit.
– Ralph Waldo Emerson –

Leaves are peeking out and stretching today, buds
are opening to the spring sun. Nature seems to be full
of joy. The word nature comes from the Latin word

nasci, which means "to be born." When my children were young, we had a picture book that described spring as the earth's birthday. So, Happy Birthday, Earth! I will celebrate by lingering with you.

25. BLUE

> Lavender's blue, dilly dilly,
> Lavender's green.
> – nursery rhyme –

This year I scattered wildflower seeds into a large planter box not knowing what might grow from them. They've been blooming over the last week, and I'm delighted to see that one of them is blue—a cornflower, aka bachelor's button. True blue seems exquisite in a flower. Hyacinths, hydrangeas, bluebells and forget-me-nots come in blue. And almost nothing matches the sight of an entire field of bluebonnets like the ones that grow in my Texas birthplace. As for the color blue itself, it comes in navy, cerulean, aqua, teal, royal blue, baby blue. And cornflower. I think I've seen the sky wear each of these blues at one time or another. Blue is a symbol of hope, so I see blue blooms as the hope-filled ones. Linger with something blue today. Linger with hope.

26. FEET

A poetry book that I read as a child had an illustration of a toddler peeking out from under a small table. I think the reason I remember that illustration is because the table was exactly like one that stood in my family's house. It had carved claw feet made of dark, polished wood. Whose claws they were supposed to be, I don't know. They were a bit feline. House cat? Lion? Tiger? I have a similar side table in my own living room now. It's smaller and once belonged to my granny. I still can't tell whose feet are on that table, but I'm guessing they were intended to be exotic.

I've been noticing all kinds of feet. On indoor furniture, there are straight feet, spindled feet, and ski-like feet on chairs that rock. On one child's stool, each foot is cupped with black rubber to protect the floors. Then there are the feet outdoors: the base of a tree, the foundation of a building, the bottom of a fence post, all places where objects touch the earth. Maybe they're overgrown with moss or ivy, maybe splashed with mud or edged by a puddle. They're places for a gathering of ants or grubs, a place for a stray white Busy Lizzy or sunflower to grow. Some feet are under the earth, like the roots that anchor trees and plants. And then there are those feet that are uniquely our own with toes and ankles and heels. All of our weight on those two feet. Amazing!

27. OURS FOR THE TAKING

Each leaf outreaching
Each bud tight curled
Each spill of blossoms
Each dewdrop pearled

Each breath of breeze
Each tangle of vine,
All of it yours,
All of it mine

For the touching
For the taking
For the waking mind.
– kh –

28. ECLECTIC

Our old couch was so well built that it is not wearing out. It once belonged to my parents and was originally covered in dark green Naugahyde with imprinted swirls of gold, a faux leather look that was popular in the 1960s. Durability was a big selling point for my parents, and they chose well. The old couch is still sturdy and comfortable, although my husband and I had it recovered in fabric.

Our house will never be a showplace. Our taste in furniture is eclectic due to a time when we were so cash-strapped that we accepted whatever furniture our parents wanted to donate to our cause. Our dining room furniture, a reddish-brown cherry wood, came from my husband's grandmother. The bedroom furniture came from my parents and is also made of reddish wood, not cherry but "solid Honduras mahogany" as the pamphlet says. Yes, I have the original pamphlet from the late 1940s or early '50s. It boasts, from the perspective of the dresser, "Romance and youth can be mine through the years" and "I have been admired for centuries" and "A jungle romance is behind my beauty secret." Such an invitation to linger!

Pause with a piece of furniture indoors or out. Notice its lines. Feel its texture. If it invites you to sit on it or pick it up or move it, and if you have time to linger longer, do.

29. NEW FLAVORS

"[C]ourse after course was brought to the table. Tender freshwater shrimp garnished with cream and rose leaves, devilled barley pearls in acorn purée, apple and carrot chews, marinated cabbage stalks steeped in creamed white turnip with nutmeg."

– Brian Jacques –

The prolific fantasy author Brian Jacques wrote for blind children and filled his books with detailed descriptions that rely on senses other than sight. He often describes detailed meals enjoyed by his main characters, who are mice. Now I've never tasted devilled barley pearls in acorn purée, but I have tried some interesting flavors. In Hong Kong, I tried lychee (which I didn't like), and in VietNam, I tried water morning glory (which I did like). I just finished a treat sent from my son in Japan: green tea Kit-Kats. A new flavor always calls me to attention. "Linger," it says. "Notice me."

30. THE WORLD AT WORK

The small room was dim. Closed curtains gently billowed in the breeze that slipped through open windows. It was naptime, and I, being a young child, was supposed to be going to sleep. But the sounds from outdoors were drifting in: the whirr of a distant lawnmower, indistinct voices, a dog barking. I was perfectly content to lie there and listen to the world at work. Even now as I move through my day, some sound will remind me to tune my ears to people at work mowing, roofing, flipping through papers, cleaning, watering, murmuring, typing on a keyboard. In mild weather, I like to open my windows and invite the sounds of the world in. Cars pass, a neighbor mows, someone saws a downed branch, lawn

sprinklers turn on across the street, a dog barks. I
linger a moment. It reminds me of naptime.

MAY

TO NOTICE SUCH THINGS

> When the Present has latched its postern
> behind my tremulous stay,
> And the May month flaps its
> glad green leaves like wings,
> Delicate-filmed as new-spun silk,
> will the neighbours say,
> He was a man who used to notice such things.
> – Thomas Hardy –

The purple-pink phlox in my front garden attracts
butterflies, and that's where I spotted one of the most
beautiful butterflies I've ever seen: a pipevine
swallowtail. Its forewings were translucent black,
veined and outlined in dark black on its leading edge
and dotted with white on the opposite edge. But the
rear, tailed wings were the show stoppers. Large white
spots ran along each outer edge, twinned with an
inner row of large orange-red spots, all on a
background of iridescent turquoise that faded to black
as it neared the butterfly's body, which was
amazing too. The front half was black covered in
small white dots.

The back half was turquoise with white dots in a line like buttons bordering the butterfly's abdomen.

Spying a butterfly is like finding a living treasure, one that's likely to flit away as quickly as it came. Each butterfly is on a journey. I usually see them when they pause for nectar. When the Present has latched its postern gate behind me, may friends and family say, "She used to notice such things."

2. FOLLOWING A WORD THREAD

I've been using the word *notice* a lot. Today I began wondering about the word itself, where it started and how knowing its origin might color my understanding of it. Looking into the origin of words feels, to me, like following a thread backward, unraveling the stitching to see where it first entered the fabric of language. Like so many other words, *notice* began ages ago in Latin with the word *notus*, which means *known*. So, to notice something is to become aware of it, to *know* it's there. I wonder how many things I pass each day without knowing they're even there, without *noticing.*

What's the first thing you notice when you step out of your door today? Notice the larger scene. What do you see, hear, and smell? Linger with it for a moment.

3. LEAVES

I planted citronella in a pot on my deck to the right of my back door. Citronella is supposed to repel mosquitoes. Basil is too. I've planted basil to the left of the door. Beyond their mosquito repelling properties, these two plants are simply all-around beautiful. Citronella grows wide. Its leaves are large and frilly and have a lemony fragrance. Basil grows thin and tall, its leaves layering the stem in a shape that reminds me of a pagoda. It has a peppery smell. I sometimes pause when I go outdoors and pinch off a bit of citronella or basil and linger with the scent. Or I might pinch off a bumpy scallop-edged leaf of fresh-scented mint, which faithfully comes back every year. Leaves are a sensory-full way to linger.

Pay attention to the leaves that attract you and fill you with wonder or joy or gratitude or peace. Rub a leaf between your fingers. Is it glossy and slick, furry, smooth, rough? Does it have a scent? To linger longer, create a bouquet made entirely of your favorite leaves.

4. A STATE OF WONDER

This past weekend, Art & Soul Nashville held an art festival. Artists with work for sale met on Saturday evening to set up their displays. Now and then, each of us would take a break and stroll around to see everyone else's artwork. It was like being in a museum. The pianist Glenn Gould once said, "The purpose of art is the lifelong construction of a state of wonder." That's the way art affects me—visual art, music, dance, theater, photography. Whether it's wildly creative, thought-provoking, exquisite, or calming, art calls me to pay attention and creates in me a sense of wonder that I can carry into every day. The extraordinary helps me see the ordinary.

5. EXTRAVAGANT GIFTS

> I stood in the Maytime meadows
> By roses circled round
> Where many a fragile blossom
> Was bright upon the ground;
> And as though the roses called them
> And their wild hearts understood,
> The little birds were singing
> In the shadows of the wood.
> – Anonymous, Medieval –

Fallen petals from a saucer magnolia carpeted the ground in magenta, pink, and white. I paused on the garden sidewalk and picked up one petal, marveling not only at its baby-soft texture but also at the way its topside was light pink, almost white, while its underside was dark pink easing into magenta.

Flowers are an astonishing wonder to me. They nod in the breeze, "Look at me!" And when I look, I see the skirts of dancers or the wings of fairies or cheerful faces turned to the sun. I see hearts of impatiens, bonnets of columbine, trumpets of mandevilla. Some petals pile in layers. Some grow shoulder to shoulder with neighboring petals. Others are separate like the arms of a star. Some arc vulnerably outward, some arc protectively inward. Some close up at night. And that's just the shape. Add color and texture and fragrance, and blooms are one of nature's most extravagant gifts.

6. A PAUSE BEFORE TASTING

Swift gratitude is the sweetest.

– Greek proverb –

When I was growing up, my family said a prayer of thanks before every meal. It taught me to pause for a moment before eating. But I've found another reason to pause before digging in: to smell and see before tasting. It seems to make a meal even more delicious. And it makes me even more grateful.

7. BIRDSONG

A bird does not sing because it has an answer.
It sings because it has a song.
– Chinese proverb –

The Carolina wren was quite cheerful this morning. She outsang the other birds with her usual clear, loud *chewy-chewy-chewy-chewy-chewy-chewy*. Birdcalls often sound like words to me. The wren sometimes changes her song to *preach-it, preach-it, preach-it*. The chickadee introduces herself with *chick-a-dee-dee-dee, chick-a-dee-dee-dee*, while her friend the tufted titmouse sings *feeder-feeder-feeder*. The white-throated sparrow croons, *where are you oh-my-love, oh-my-love, oh-my-love?* And the blue jay squawks, *Hey! Hey! Hey!* I've yet to discover which bird is singing *Rock-City, Rock-City, Rock-City*. Or the one that calls *cheeseburger-cheeseburger-cheeseburger*.

8. RED

When I was little, my dad taught me how to clean my room by making it a game. "I'll leave the room for two minutes," he'd say. "I won't peek. See if you can pick up everything that's red before I come back." He would leave, and I would scurry around, plucking up the toys that were red. When he came back, he would check and repeat the challenge with another color, then another and another until the room was clean.

So that's my challenge to myself today, not by cleaning but by noticing shades and hues of red from bright red to vermillion to crimson to maroon. I plan to let red call to me today.

9. MOVING WATER

One of my youngest grandson's favorite walks at Cheekwood Botanical Gardens leads to a fountain in a small pond of water lilies. It's one of the most peaceful places in the gardens. I think it's the sound of the fountain that initially calls to us, but we're also attracted by the dance of the bubbling water atop the large stone pedestal in the center. Sun-sparkled water burbles up and flows down across the sides of the carved stone pedestal. We linger, sitting on the retaining wall, watching, fascinated as water splashes into the pond below, sending ripples through the pooled water, gently rocking the water lilies.

10. KITCHEN SYMPHONY

The chosen pan clatters out of the cabinet,
scraping against those left behind,
clunks onto the burner,
clicks as it heats,
hisses to onions and green peppers
that answer with a sizzle.
Across the room,
glasses clink,
silverware jangles,
wooden spoons whisk and stir.
The microwave hums for a moment,
then beeps.

The kitchen's a symphony
that starts with an overture—
allegro, staccato,
crescendo to forte.
Now a decrescendo to
dinner hour,
andante, mezzo forte,
ascending laughter,
descending murmurs,
a scrape, a clank,
a rattle, a tap.

Then another crescendo to the grand finale
that moves to the sink—
the thunk of a trashcan,
the splash of rinsewater,
the swish of a dishbrush.
Plates and silverware come to the fore,
clatter into the dishwasher.
The door snaps shut,
the dishwasher purrs.
Mezzo piano.
Fermata,
Decrescendo,
Ritard,
Piano,
Piano,
Pianissimo,
Finé.
– kh –

11. NEGATIVE SPACE

I once had a kaleidoscope with a shallow, snap-on disk that fit on the end. You could remove it, peel back its lid, and place different small objects inside: paper clips, petals, bits of paper, seeds. Then you popped it back on to see the patterns the different items made. Part of the pattern was the negative space, the blank space between objects. I sometimes think of that kaleidoscope when I look at trees and branches, or more accurately at the patterns of negative space where the sky shows between the leaves and branches. I once took a drawing class where one assignment was to sketch a plant or tree by drawing only the negative spaces. The point was to nudge my mind to see what's really there instead of what I think is there. So here I am today, lingering with the awesomeness of negative space.

12. SMALL, BUSY, WINGED THINGS

Drifting about among flowers and sunshine,
I am like a butterfly or bee,
though not half so busy or with so sure an aim.
– John Muir –

Butterflies, bees, airplane bugs, moths, fireflies, cicadas—when one of these small, busy, winged creatures lands nearby, pause and watch it for a moment. Marvel at the tiny precision of its design, its colors and patterns, its wings and feelers and feet.

13. SACRED GIFT

> In every walk with Nature
> one receives far more than he seeks.
> – John Muir –

Nature is a sacred gift, wild and precious, a treasure to fully experience with all our senses, to really see and hear, not to rush and brush aside but to linger and wonder and be grateful.

14. DESCRIBING ONE SENSE WITH ANOTHER

> I would like to paint the way a bird sings.
> – Claude Monet –

Monet has a fascinating way of comparing a visual medium to a sound, which seems to me a very artistic thing to do. I've heard some singers described as having a smoky voice, equating a sound with a description that's both a scent and a visual. Once a writing teacher questioned my use of color and shape to describe a smell: the round golden aroma of creamy soup. True, that may sound strange, but that's the way I think of the fragrance of creamy soup.

It's round. Sometimes when you linger, those are the impressions you get.

15. SMOOTH AND ROUGH

I just glanced out the window and saw my neighbor sanding the rail on top of his deck stairs. I think he's getting it ready to repaint. When I was nine years old, I used rough scraps of wood to build a child size vanity table for my younger sister's birthday. It needed sanding before I could paint it. Since I'd never sanded anything before, I didn't realize the job would require so much "elbow grease," as my grandmother would say. I stuck at it for as long as I could. The final product was inconsistent in texture and a bit lopsided, but I painted it metallic gold, which seemed to make up for the rough, lopsided look. In fact, the gold paint made it magical.

Run your fingertips over something rough and some-thing smooth. Linger a moment with the feel of each.

16. INTO ETERNAL MYSTERY

Linger,
heart open,
intent on the smallest bit
of nature's art—
a pebble,

a butterfly,
a bud,
raindrops;
let wonder widen,
dreams deepen,
hopes stretch and soar
up and out and into
the eternal mystery
that many call
God.

– kh –

17. CHANGES

The course of Nature is the art of God.
– Edward Young –

In Nashville, street speed limits were recently lowered to 25 miles per hour in neighborhoods. That's a change from 30 and 35. The lower speed is not only safer, it's also more conducive to noticing changes that are happening along the routes I take to the grocery store, to the art studio, to my hair stylist's salon, or to my son's house. There's a lot of road work and construction going on, but those aren't really the changes I'm thinking of. I'm thinking of the grander changes that happen day by day, season by season in the course of nature. Winter branches and bare lawns sprout leaves and flowers. Spring blossoms fade, making way for summer's deep green and the flowers that thrive in hotter weather. Rains come and go. Winds drift and shift and blow. And we are witnesses to these changes.

But not only are we witnesses, we're also participants. The seasons of our lives tend to follow the seasons of nature. Our lives have a spring, a summer, an autumn, and if we live long enough, a winter. We witness that, too. We follow the course of nature. We are the art of God.

18. THE MAGIC

The sun is shining—the sun is shining.
That is the Magic.
The flowers are growing—the roots are stirring.
That is the Magic.
Being alive is the Magic—
being strong is the Magic.
The Magic is in me—the Magic is in me. . . .
It's in every one of us.
– Frances Hodgson Burnett –

On one wall of my sunroom there hangs a decorative plaque that says, "Be still and know that I am." It's a Bible verse, originally said by God. I think it means, "Be still and rest in the fact that I exist." Or, "Linger and feel my existence." Sometimes I apply it to myself, telling myself to be still and know that I exist, to linger with the reality of my own existence. Feel my own heart beating. Listen to myself breathing. Feel life flowing through me. "Being alive is the Magic—being strong is the Magic. The Magic is in me—the Magic is in me. . . . It's in every one of us."

19. BUBBLES

This morning when I poured my coffee, I noticed the bubbles that form on the surface of the coffee. They winked back at me in tiny reflections of light, and as I lingered there, looking at them, I realized the light they were reflecting was the shape of my window. In fact, each bubble held an exact reflection of the window. I also realized that this happens every day when I pour my coffee. I had only just now noticed it.

One of my most distinct memories of childhood is of bubbles in the form of suds at a friend's house as we washed dishes. I remember the joy of sticking my hands in the bubbles, noticing how the light reflected off of them, how they felt soft and soapy and squishy, how they smelled crisply clean, how they fizzed and popped.

Bubbles are fascinating. If you have time, pause with some today in your own coffee or in dish liquid, bubble bath, soda fizz, bubble gum—or even blowing bubbles. Watch for reflections and colors, feel the texture, listen to the fizz. Linger.

20. A Dozen Names for Rain

The thirsty earth soaks up the rain,
And drinks, and gapes for drink again.
– Abraham Cowley –

Rain is drumming down this morning, steady and heavy. I've had to close the windows on the west side of the house, so I know it's blowing in from the west as it often does. The weather forecast predicted showers, but this is more than a shower. What would I call it? There are at least a dozen names for rain: shower, sprinkle, squall, sheets, drizzle, torrent, deluge, downpour, gully washer (or window washer, depending on where you come from), cloudburst, drencher, and my favorite, sun-shower. Drencher sounds about right today.

The next time it rains, linger with it. You may come up with a new name for rain.

21. RAPT

One of the dictionary definitions of wonder is "rapt attention," and it's my favorite because "rapt" means "lifted up and carried away." Wonder lifts up our souls and carries them away into awe and delight and gratitude. Wonder nourishes our souls. We may have to slow down and pause and linger, but whatever path we're on in life, there's something worth our rapt attention. My challenge for myself today is to find one aspect of nature to which I can give rapt attention.

22. UNDERFOOT

On the way back to my house from my curbside mailbox today, cradling a stack of catalogues, bills, and one bubble wrap envelope, I paused at the one large, flat stepping stone that crosses our narrow front garden. I had been thinking that what's underfoot often goes unnoticed, so I squatted and eyed the mottled brown-and-gray, uneven stone. A few dull yellow-green leaves were scattered across it, and because of an earlier rain, the dips in the stone were small puddles. They probably seemed like large ponds from the perspective of an ant, who crawled around the perimeter of one of the smaller leaves. She disappeared underneath. Maybe the leaf looked like a tent to her. Then a fly landed near one of the puddles, rubbed its face with its forefeet, and took off again. I ran my finger over the rough stone. Then I dug into the soggy leaf mulch beside it, just for the tactile pleasure of it.

As I stood again, I saw that the rock was longer on the left side and tapered to its right, which made it a bit heart-shaped if I angled my head just so. On the other hand, having spent the day with my preschool grandson, I had to admit that the rock looked more like the skull of a dinosaur.

23. THE AIR, IN PASSING

The feathered race with pinions skim the air.
– John Hookham Frere –

As I read this quote by the poet Frere, I thought, wait—we skim the air too, even though we don't often pay attention to the way air passes around our bodies as we move. It's easier to feel in warm weather when our arms are bare. I'm not talking about winds and breezes when we're outdoors. This sensation comes indoors as we move around. I first noticed it as I walked up the stairs in my house. A gentle, cool breeziness brushes my arms. It's not because the air is blowing past me; it's because I'm passing through the air. It's so gentle, I rarely notice it. If I could see the air around me—if it were a colored mist—I suspect I would see swirls and waves, upward drifts and downward dips. But as it's invisible, it's the unseen, airy art of me being in the world.

24. IN THE CENTER

A flower is an invitation
to wonder,
to marvel,
to love,
to linger,
to dream,
to blossom,
to be glad,
to hope,
to delight,
to remember,
to pause and begin again.
– kh –

For me, one of the delights of lingering with flowers is leaning close enough to see their centers. My white mandevillas have bright yellow throats as if they drank sunlight. My coneflowers have pincushion-looking centers. In the center of each of my zinnias, there's a small collection of tiny, golden-yellow flowers—flowers within the flower. And the center of my white phalaenopsis orchid looks like the face of a small, magenta-spotted leopard. Each flower is like a sacred space, a small temple, and this is its inner sanctum, its holy of holies, its invitation to linger.

25. SUNSETS

As I've noted before, I grew up in West Texas, where the land is flat, the sky is big, and the horizon is a stark, straight line between earth and sky, uninterrupted by hills or trees or even buildings. Sunsets create a flamboyant display of colors in the western sky, every night different as the setting sun paints with an unlimited palette of colors. Blue often pales to green, then turns gold before deepening into a fiery orange that stretches up and out and becomes a ribbon of crimson softening into lavender, turquoise, and a rich blue that darkens as the overhead sky spreads out its evening cloak of deep violet-black sparked with stars.

Here in Tennessee, we usually can't see such brilliant big-sky sunsets, but as the sun sinks, I often look out the window to see a bright red-gold burst of sunlight breaking through an opening between trees to the west. Or I glance up from reading and see a striking green glowing through leaves of honeysuckle, stippled by a more muted, darker green of leaf shadow on leaf. Then there are times when after-storm clouds catch the fiery red of the sunset and turn it into such flashy pinks and golds that cars slow and pedestrians stop, and everyone pauses at the same time to gaze at this free light show, this gift of the setting sun.

26. WHITE

Blow trumpet, for the world is white with May.

– Alfred, Lord Tennyson –

I'm gathering white for my soul today. The white of newly blooming, perfumed magnolias. The white of dandelions ready to sail away on the breeze. The white of a friend's moonflower that, at the moment, is curled into a whorl waiting to fully open tonight. The white of billowing clouds. The white of snowdrop windflowers bobbing in the breeze. The white of indoor orchids blooming again. The white of a new ream of printer paper. The white of softly scented baby powder. The white of a freshly gessoed canvas. The white of lotion that smells like cherry blossoms. The white of a lampshade. The white of this new page on my laptop, waiting to be filled with these words.

27. THE BIG PICTURE

With hues on hues
expression cannot paint
The breath of Nature,
And her endless bloom.
– James Thomson –

Sometimes I'm so focused on noticing the small details of nature that I forget to take in the big picture. I'm drawn to the tiered petals of emerging irises or the elegance of hosta blooms or the structure of the winglike leaves on the new basil plant. Once in a while, I have to remind myself to notice the big picture, to stand back and take in the whole view. It helps to actually take a step back and squint as I look at a garden or a flower stall or the floral or produce section in the supermarket. Squinting helps me skip the detail and get my impression of the view. Where's the darkest area? Where's the lightest? What's the overall color? Where do I notice splashes of color, maybe one that surprises me? It's possible to do the same using other senses, listening for the dominant sound, smelling the most pervasive aroma, letting my skin comment on the feel of the world at present, its temperature, its dryness or humidity, its breeziness or stillness. Pause to get a momentary overall impression of a place today.

28. EYES

The eyes are the window of the soul.
– 16th century proverb –

I don't know if that proverb refers to looking out from your own eyes or looking into someone else's eyes. It could mean that through my own eyes, what I see reveals my own soul. Author Steven Covey wrote, "What you see often depends on what you are looking for." On the other hand, the proverb could mean that when I look at someone's eyes, something of their soul is revealed. Truly, the proverb could apply both to looking out and to looking in.

I've always been drawn to eyes. It's what I notice most about a person. When I draw or paint a portrait, I try to catch what the person seems to be expressing, what they're feeling or thinking. Eyes are expressive and endlessly fascinating, their shape, their colors, the glint of light reflected in them. I enjoy noticing these windows of the soul.

29. SOAP

My youngest grandson is pumping a generous amount of liquid hand soap onto his palms. Both of his palms. One will not do. His pleasure with that small task of handwashing reminds me to pay attention to the slick feel of soap, its fresh scent, its bubbly froth in the water. I wash my hands a lot these days. The practice has become so commonplace that I easily overlook the sensory experience of it. My grandson is now offering me the soap. I pump a generous amount onto my right palm. Then—why not—onto the left palm as well. We are awash in soap bubbles today.

30. SUNDAY MORNING SOUNDS

Nobody started it, nobody is going to stop it.
It will talk as long as it wants, this rain.
As long as it talks I am going to listen.
– Thomas Merton –

I stand at the back door, holding it open for the cat as she decides whether or not she wants to venture out into the sprinkling rain. A hummingbird settles at his feeder only six feet away. He dips his long, sharp beak into the sugar water, then sits back watchful before taking another sip. Nearby in the yard, a chipmunk chip-chip-chips. In the dripping trees, birds call good morning—cardinals, sparrows, titmice, chickadees, each with its own chirp or warble or whistle.

The cat finally decides not to brave the shower and ducks back indoors. I stand for a minute longer, listening to the soft patter of rain, enjoying the cooler air that comes with it. Then I, too, duck inside.

31. STEP OUTDOORS

To the attentive eye, each moment of the year
has its own beauty,
and in the same field it beholds, every hour,
a picture which was never seen before,

and which shall never be seen again.
– Ralph Waldo Emerson –

As I step outside my door today, I glance around to see how the scene has changed from earlier in this month. What's different? Is there a new feel in the air? A new scent? The days are warmer now that our part of the earth has tilted more toward the sun. The sky, of course, is always different. Today it's blue overhead, but clouds are piled up and peeking over the treetops. They're bright white brushed with gray, which makes me hope for rain for my garden. Each day, there seems to be something new in bloom. Today it's a brick-orange daylily with a bright yellow throat. And while we've had wild violets in the yard for a while, they've been joined by white clover blossoms, which means I'll probably see bees soon. Emerson has reminded me that this is a picture which was never seen before, and which shall never be seen again.

JUNE

MEASURING

An artist friend and I pulled a length of white paper from a large roll. She measured it with her forearm—one, two, three, four lengths. We were hanging paper as a backdrop for an art show, and it had to be long enough, top to bottom, to cover a section of wall. Her arm-measuring reminded me of the way I often measure a length of thread when I'm preparing to sew a handmade pillowslip or mend a hem or replace a missing button. I pull thread off the spool to about the length of my forearm. It's not precise, but it's good enough for the task at hand. Measuring is a tactile experience, whether I estimate the amount of salt by pouring it into my hand or measure it exactly in a teaspoon.

Life itself is not so easily measured. Rabbi Danya Ruttenberg recently posted a challenging thought online: "How would you like to measure your life? Maybe you can do one thing in the next 24 hours that reflects *that*?" Yes. Yes, maybe I can.

2. CLOUD NINE

> I am the daughter of Earth and Water,
> And the nursling of the Sky.
> I pass through the pores of the ocean and shores;
> I change, but I cannot die.
> – Percy Bysshe Shelley, "The Cloud" –

I only recently found out why we say that someone is "on cloud nine" when they're especially happy. In 1896, a manual was published that helped people identify types of clouds. Ten classes of clouds were listed, the cumulonimbus being ninth on the list. As it happens, cumulonimbus clouds can stretch up as far as ten miles, which makes them the tallest of all the clouds. Gavin Pretor-Pinney, founder of the Cloud Appreciation Society, describes the cumulonimbus as "the monumental architecture of air." So someone "on cloud nine" is monumentally high on happiness.

3. MISTY MOISTY

> One misty moisty morning
> When cloudy was the weather . . .

That's the way an old nursery rhyme starts, one that my mother used to repeat on misty moisty mornings like this. This morning, those lines are whispering to me as I look out my bedroom window. A cloud has landed on the ground. The view of trees one block over has been whitened and softened, blurred in fog. Drips fall in slow plops from the trees. Droplets line the bottom edge of the window screen like sequins strung by fairies during the night. Quiet feathery air and a hush of mist soften the edges of the world today.

4. UNDERNEATH

I moved a flower pot today and disturbed the world underneath it, the domain of little gray-brown creatures we used to call doodle bugs and pill bugs and roly-polies. The armored bodies with their many legs skittered away to find a new hiding place. I picked one up, watching it curl into a ball. It unrolled itself in my palm and trundled across my hand with its fourteen legs. Under rocks, logs, fallen limbs, and leaves is the small, busy world of ants, earthworms, beetles, grubs, and doodle bugs. It's a tiny world I used to watch often when I was a child. It's a tiny world worth noticing even now.

5. IN BETWEEN

> The notes I handle no better than many pianists.
> But the pauses between the notes—
> ah, that is where the art resides.
> – Artur Schnabel, pianist and composer –

Today was an open-windows day, the kind of day that's perfect for mopping the kitchen floor, since it dries faster in a warm breeze. It's a task I had been putting off for weeks, so the job was past due. The only hitch was that my preschool grandson was here, so that meant interruptions, or to look at it another way, pauses. I divided the floor into quadrants and mopped one quadrant, then paused to take a good look at a restaurant my grandson was building out of blocks. I mopped the second quadrant before pausing to watch the dance of a toy Lego snake, powered by an energetic little boy. The day's tasks are punctuated with pauses, which is just fine. It's these pauses that really matter in the end.

What's on your to-do list today? Try to pause between tasks. Stretch, breathe, linger. Feel the end of one task and the beginning of another. Notice the moment. We need the space between thoughts, between steps, between notes, between words, between now and next.

6. GATES

Our next-door neighbors just finished building a gate made of bamboo that grows in the canebrake between their yard and ours. They built it to keep in a new dog. But it's also the perfect entrance to their backyard, which is landscaped like an Asian garden with a rock path, a bench, and ginger plants with large tropical leaves and clusters of pale yellow blooms that smell amazing.

Gates are intriguing. Depending on which side you're on, they can be an entrance or an exit. Sometimes that difference matters. Gates invite us in or keep us out. They stand guard. They lead somewhere. Enter or exit, and you've crossed a line into a different space, although it may only be between the front and back yard. Notice the gates you pass by—or through—today.

7. WILDFLOWERS

They're starting to bloom: my mystery flowers, my surprise plants, the wildflowers I scattered in a large planter on my deck. Every spring for years, I've been tempted to buy a packet of mixed wildflowers just to see what grows. This year I finally did. But I had no idea what was going to emerge. Now I know: blue, ragged-edged cornflowers; a white bloom mottled in purple—lemon bee balm; a tiny white flower with a yellow "outie" in the center—eastern black nightshade; a small pink bloom called sweet William catchfly; a bright sunflower; and a small purple larkspur.

Many wildflowers are so small that I have to lean close to see them. Like chickweed. Or wild strawberry. Or pink thoroughwart. If these blooms were large, they would be considered spectacular. As it is, their greatest admirers seem to be ants and bees, ladybugs and spiders—and now me.

8. THE PEPPERS

We went for pancake mix,
but halfway down the market aisle,
my preschool grandson paused
before a bin of bell peppers
placed at exactly his height,
sorted by color,
and shiny as jewels.
Red
Yellow
Orange
Green

"Look!" He picked up a red one,
then yellow, then orange.
I picked up a green pepper.
They were smooth as glass,
inviting as crayons,
and we were artists.
"They're amazing," I said,
"But we don't need peppers today."
Although in fact,
we did.
– kh –

9. SUNLIGHT

Glowing golden,
pouring in
through windowpanes
and cracks and veins
of leaves and boughs
and splashing down
the trunks of trees,
the warm light of dawn.
– kh –

The sun is an artist beginning her day with a pastel palette and painting only the tip-top leaves of the hackberry, the poplar, the elms. Her pink-gold light trickles down the tree trunks like a slow-motion waterfall that brightens the tree as it goes and makes leaves glow as if they hold an inner light all their own.

By noon, the sun is pouring her colors over roofs, roads, fields, rivers and lakes. She saturates flowers with colors that shout. But then she angles a bit and backs off, slowly edging toward the west as she turns her attention toward her next canvas. Shadows lengthen as she sinks toward the horizon. Her light reverses its morning brush strokes, ebbing up tree trunks until at last, only the tip-top leaves of the hackberry, the poplar, and the elm glow green-gold. Then they, too, are left in shadow.

10. SUMMER SOUNDTRACK

Listen.
Listen past the noise
to softer sounds.
Wind, water,
bugs, birdsong,
a church bell, a distant train.
Listen
to your own deep breath
drifting in and out.
Listen as the sounds of peace
calm your soul.
– kh –

The old frame house in the mountains of North Carolina was a perfect place for a retreat. A group of writer friends and I shared the expense to rent it for a week. We spent most of our time silent, thinking and writing with the sounds of the woods as our soundtrack. The old house itself gave us creaks, groans, and unidentifiable scritches and scratches. (A raccoon on the roof? A squirrel? A possum? This was dinner conversation.) Other sounds were pure delight. Wind swishing through trees. A stream rushing downhill around rocks and fallen limbs. And frogs. I've never heard such a chorus of frogs garumphing and croaking and chirruping and crooning. This was our nightly lullabye.

Pause to listen to the sounds of summer.

TODAY'S GRAND SHOW

This grand show is eternal.
It is always sunrise somewhere . . .
a shower is forever falling;
vapor is ever rising.
Eternal sunrise, eternal sunset,
eternal dawn and gloaming,
on sea and continents and islands,
each in its turn,
as the round earth rolls.
– John Muir –

Linger with the grand show that is today.

12. IN THE BACK YARD UNDER THE PINES

I meant to put on sunscreen,
insect repellent,
maybe even a floppy hat—
isn't that how you dress
for a garden that needs weeding?
Instead, I went out to take a picture
of a rose,
the first of the season.
Then the mahonia beckoned,
its berries hanging in grape-like clusters,
blue powdered with white,
another photo op
in the back yard under the pines
in the garden that needed weeding.

I'll just test the weeds, I thought,
see if recent rains have softened the soil,
find out if they pull easily.
Up came a mat of chickweed,
a clump of wild violets,
tendrils of ivy,
all overstretching their bounds.
And so it went,
tugging and tossing,
freeing the spent daffodils
from one clump of weeds,

then another
and another.

There on my knees,
fingers digging through pine straw,
I breathe the rich smell of dirt,
the fresh scent of leaves.
A surprised millipede skitters past,
disturbed earthworms tunnel deeper.
Chickadees sing their name,
wrens chirr,
a woodpecker tap-tap-taps overhead.
The wind brushes and shushes
the pines and elms,
ebbing and flowing like the ocean,
a sea of air
swishing,
sighing,
whispering peace—
peace with the rhythms of nature,
peace with the seasons of life and death
in the garden, now in late spring bloom
after dying back for winter.

Whispering, too, of my own seasons,
of my own dying to come
some day.
Even though I hear the whisper,
even though I might prepare,

that day will surprise me.
Oh—
I meant to put on sunscreen,
insect repellent,
a floppy hat—
isn't that how you dress for a garden?
– kh –

13. IN BACK OF A BLOOM

Flowers put their painted faces forward, whether they boldly look out and up into the spotlight of the sun or demurely bow their heads. They're photogenic that way. But the backs of flowers are interesting too. They have their own beauty. With the sun in their faces, their petals viewed from the back are often translucent, and their veins, sometimes a darker color, are easier to see. Some blooms, like the yellow helenium, are just as bright on the underside as on top. Others, like the zinnia, are light green or buff on the underside even though they're bright orange, red, or yellow on top. It takes a bit of lingering to notice the underside of flowers, but they reward us when we do.

14. BUZZ AND CHIRP

A chorus of buzzing insects is making the whole world feel drowsy today and is conjuring memories of my slower paced childhood. Summer afternoons ran late and long. Evening brought a light show of fireflies and the songs of crickets. In West Texas, we had glossy black crickets. Jiminy crickets. They would often show up indoors. We didn't mind watching them or catching them; they were friendly crickets. I've learned that you can figure out the temperature by counting a cricket's chirps. The *Old Farmer's Almanac* says to count the number of chirps in fourteen seconds, then add forty to get the temperature. "For example: 30 chirps + 40 = 70°F." So I guess if it's hot, they chirp faster. I move slower.

Pause if you hear insects. Listen to their drowsy song.

15. LOOKING WITH QUIET EYES

I will be the gladdest thing
Under the sun!
I will touch a hundred flowers
And not pick one.

I will look at cliffs and clouds
With quiet eyes,
Watch the wind bow down the grass,
And the grass rise. . . .
– Edna St. Vincent Millay –

I invite you to join me as I look with quiet eyes today. Notice what piques your interest and linger with it.

16. WHAT SLOWS US DOWN

The author Mitali Perkins wrote on her social media that two things slow her down and "invite [her] to dwell in the moment": deadheading spent blossoms and brushing her dog. In response, her friends shared what slows them down. On the list are cleaning crevices like grout and pulling weeds from cracks in a walkway. For me it's watering plants, folding clothes and putting them away, and walking to the mailbox at the curb to check my mail. Some tasks call us to linger, take a deep breath, and check in with all our senses.

17. SUMMER STARS

The sun's rim dips; the stars rush out;
At one stride comes the dark
– Samuel Taylor Coleridge –

Summer stargazing is different from winter stargazing. I didn't really notice this until my sons were young and we started watching the night sky. One reason summer stargazing is different is because days are longer, so stars appear later. Also, the summer sky is hazier, because it holds more moisture, so it's thicker and dims the starlight. In winter, the sky is crisper and clearer, making stars appear brighter. But the main difference is that because Earth is always circling the sun, we're on the opposite side of the sun in summer from where we are in winter. So we actually see different stars and constellations. While lots of faint stars in the Milky Way are visible in summer, the really bright stars show up in winter. Still, there's usually always something grand and interesting going on in the heavens. Linger with the night sky when you can.

18. SIDEWALKS

The place to observe nature is where you are:
the walk to take to-day is the walk

you took yesterday.
You will not find just the same things.
– John Burroughs –

Last Sunday, the weather was on the edge of too hot, but I walked to church anyway. I walk as often as I can. For the first block, I walk on grass, and then there's a sidewalk the rest of the way. It's an ordinary concrete sidewalk, cracked in places, but this two-block stretch is unique, as every stretch of sidewalk is, and I think of it as mine. I feel the seasons along this path. I watch the trees grow thick with summer leaves. I watch the sky change. I see what wildflowers grow along the sidewalk's edge and in its cracks. When I was ten, I slow-walked along the sidewalk that led to Granny's house after school, because my eyes were on whatever book I was reading. Now I slow-walk along the sidewalk because my eyes are on the sidewalk and the world it's taking me through.

19. SIMPLICITY

The art of art, the glory of expression . . . is simplicity.
– Walt Whitman –

It's the simple things that deeply nourish my soul. My grandson's smile. The laughter of friends. A pepper turning red on the vine. The dance of leaves in a breeze on a hot day. The sun shining red through a broad canna leaf. The scent of citronella leaves at the back door. The prickly center of a coneflower. The smooth texture and hint of sweetness in coconut yogurt. The chirring of a wren as it guards its nest box. Simple, sacred gifts, each creating a stir of wonder, each offering inner peace.

20. FLOWER NAMES

Noticing often leads me to wonder. As I watered my impatiens this week, I wondered about their name. Impatiens. It sounds a lot like impatience, which I figured couldn't be right, because these are bountiful, colorful blooms that patiently survive my haphazard gardening. As it turns out, I was wrong. That's exactly what the name means: impatient. It seems that the seed pods "discharge forcibly at a slight touch," an explosive trait I've never noticed before. (They obviously do this quietly and on the sly. I plan to do the slight-touch test when pods form later in the season.) I've learned that zinnias were named for a German botanist whose last name was Zinn. Sunflowers were named for the way they turn their faces to the sun. Tulips were named by someone who thought they looked like turbans, which in Persia were called dulbands. That obviously went through a few twists and turns to become tulip.

What's your favorite flower? If you don't know how it got its name, maybe you can pause sometime and look it up.

21. A WINDOW INTO SUMMER

One touch of nature makes the whole world kin.
– John Muir –

Linger at the window you chose to use as a frame (see January 19). How has the scene changed from spring? As a reminder: If your view is a nature scene, let it be a sacred space, a small revelation of nature. If your view is a building or other structure, let it be a small tribute to shapes, textures, and shadows. Either way, it's a unique view just for you.

22. WINDSONG

The wind is blowing through the trees, and I'm wondering how to describe the sound. It's not the first time I've wondered this. Several years ago, I wrote a set of novels in which the wind is almost a character. I spent a lot of time pondering the sound of wind brushing past leaves. Other sounds have words that describe them in a satisfying way. A brook babbles. Lightning crackles. Thunder rumbles or growls or booms. But the specific sound of wind through leaves? I know wind rages, whistles, dances, shoves, drifts, whirls, and sighs. But what's the sound it makes rustling leaves? Rustle is close but not quite right. Rush? Shush? Whisper? That's as close as I can come for now. I'm still listening.

23. FEEDING BIRDS

> Black-capped chickadee,
> if I hold out seeds for you,
> will you come to me?
> – kh –

Chickadees are one of my favorite birds. They're small and friendly and quite distinct with their black heads and chins and their gray backs. They're not afraid to visit my bird feeder when I'm sitting nearby, so one day I decided to see if one would eat out of my hand. I sat very still and held out a palm full of sunflower seeds. One chickadee perched nearby but never came all the way to my hand.

Another favorite is the nuthatch. They eat upside down. Yesterday, I was filling my birdfeeder with seeds as a nuthatch watched from a branch not far away. Since my bird feeder is high on a hook, I use a pole to lift it down to the deck. I thought that would scare away the nuthatch, but he kept watching. After I filled the feeder, I picked it back up with the pole, but before I could return it to its hook, the nuthatch flew to the feeder and, upside down, pecked around for a seed. I stood

still, holding out the feeder until the nuthatch had found
a seed to his liking and had flown away again.

Pause to watch a bird today.

24. EVENING

> It is a beauteous evening, calm and free.
> – William Wordsworth –

It was the fireflies that caused me to pause as I was
closing the blinds at the window tonight. They're
rising like flickering flames in the dark, making yards
up and down the street look like twinkling fairy
kingdoms. I want to slow time so I can absorb this real
life magical moment, to bottle this summer evening to
open it later like a fine wine on some cold, dark
winter night. Maybe that's what lingering is. Maybe
it's our effort to slow time.

25. IN CHILDHOOD

As a child, I was fascinated by the way water flowed
onto the concrete driveway when our lawn was
watered. I followed the leading edge of the stream as it
slowly rolled down the driveway toward the street
leaving a dark, soaked trail behind it. I watched ants and
land snails and worms. I tasted honeysuckle and
listened to mockingbirds, stroked the bellies of horned
toads, and smelled new-mown grass. Then I grew up

and went for days without paying much attention to the natural world. Until I had children. Then I began to see it again. I found that the more I practice lingering, the more natural it becomes for me to notice the present moment the way I did in childhood.

26. ACROSS A LAWN

On the way to my mailbox, I bend down and run my hand over a patch of lawn, which is only partially grass. There are also ruffled wild violet leaves that bloomed in the spring; soft, lobed clover leaves with white blossoms; and today for the first time, I'm seeing tiny, lavender-pink liriope blooms. Liriope, also known as monkey grass, grows in the narrow strip of garden between my driveway and my neighbor's. There, it's tall and leafy. My neighbor planted it. In contrast, the small blooms on my lawn are thin and short, and they planted themselves. Still, they're pretty, and I'm happy to have them among the grass, violets, and clover.

27. NATURE'S SKYLINE

The windows in front of my desk look out on a skyline of trees. I close one eye for better focus, and with my forefinger, I trace that skyline in the air, following the tops of the trees as they curve and link, rise and dip, angle and bend. It occurs to me that if I were actually drawing this line on paper, it would look like a map with the sky as the sea and this treeline as a coastline with peninsulas and inlets and coves and one big bay. But my finger is only tracing a sea of air and a coastline of trees.

28. CLEAN AND DIRTY

> All clean and comfortable
> I sit down to write.
> – John Keats –

There's nothing like the fresh feeling of stepping out of the shower and toweling off, clean all over. On the other hand, I find a certain delight in the feel of grabbing a handful of paint and flinging it onto paper, unconcerned about getting it on my face or hair or arms or feet. One of the happiest chapters of my life was taking a pottery class, hands in clay and slip, kicking the wheel and free to come home muddy from head to toe. What does clean feel like? What does messy and dirty feel like? Linger with one or the other—or both—and notice how you feel. To me, each feels like a different kind of free.

29. CURVES

Yesterday I went to a wedding. The bride, the groom, and the pastor stood centered at the front of the sanctuary, framed by a high, wide, arched opening in the wall beyond them, which also framed a tall window farther back. The curve of the arch seemed like a gentle bow of protection, a blessing over the wedding.

Curves seem soft somehow. Instead of a full-steam-ahead straight line, a curve takes off to the side, sightseeing. It rounds a corner with an invitation to follow. At the wedding, the steps up into the reception hall were curved. The wedding cake was tiers of curves. At home now, my hand fits perfectly over the curve in the arm of the chair I'm sitting in. Through the window, I can see the upward curve of elm branches and the gentle downward curve of a crape myrtle loaded with blooms. The base of a lamp, the handle of a water pitcher, the cat's back as she sits at the window, the waning moon outdoors—all are curves. Pause to notice curves today.

30. THE SAME BUT DIFFERENT

I found every breath of air, and every scent,
And every flower and leaf and blade of grass,
And every passing cloud, and everything in nature,
More beautiful and wonderful to me
Than I had ever found it yet.
– Charles Dickens –

Dickens gave this bit of dialogue to his character Esther Summerson in Bleak House. She had been ill, so when she recovered, she found that her view of the ordinary things around her had changed. I once took a writing workshop on description in which we were asked to describe a setting as if we were angry or depressed. Then we were asked to describe the same setting as if we were happy and excited. The point was that when a character is happy, stairs may look like an exciting invitation into adventure. When the same character is sad or depressed, those same stairs may look weathered and creaky and dangerous. When she's happy, she sees dandelions as flowers. When she's depressed, she sees them as weeds. Of course, that writing exercise was based on real life. Our emotions affect whether we see roses or thorns. It's not a bad practice to notice how our emotions color what we experience when we linger.

SUMMER

JULY

1. FULL

The suffix –*ful* is whispering to me today as in wonderful, thankful, beautiful. Because -*ful* is so common, I use it without thinking about it. Everyone knows that, very simply, -*ful* means full of whatever-it-is. But lingering with –*ful*, I'm see it a bit deeper: wonder full, thank full, peace full, joy full, meaning full, beauty full, hope full. Full is not just on the surface but through and through. Full of wonder. Full of thanks. Full of peace. Full of joy. Full of meaning. Full of beauty. Full of hope. Full. Full is abundant. It can easily spill out and overflow. So . . . now my heart is full.

2. NATURE'S WAY

Little Virginia spiderwort,
three blue petals with tiny yellow stamen,
I saw you growing wild,
on my path to church this morning.
I noticed how you had crept out
from the hedge beside the road,
how you were open to the day,
fresh and new.
I thought of pausing,

of taking a closer look,
taking your picture,
but I told myself that on my return,
I would pass this way again.
I would take your picture later.

After only an hour and a half,
I was on my way home,
phone in hand,
ready to snap your picture.
And there you were.
But you had curled up your petals
to protect yourself
from the heat of the day.
I understand.
That's nature's way.
With the sun hot on my head,
I put away my phone
and turn toward home.
– kh –

3. REPETITION

In a *New York Times* article titled "My Secret Weapon Against the Attention Economy," Elliott Holt wrote, "Repetition cultivates a deeper kind of attention." He was talking about listening to the repetition of words in poetry, but I also applied it to nature. There's not just one hydrangea but a whole bush full; not just one petal but three, four, five, dozens. One finch comes to the feeder, then five more flock in. I notice one bee on the mint blossoms. When I look closer, I see another. And then another. When a bird calls, it repeats its melody over and over and often gets an echoing call in return from a more distant bird. Once in a while, I notice a lone falcon, a single goldfinch, a solitary stray acorn, one cloud in the sky. But nature usually presents us with an abundance of repetition. Nature is generous like that. Maybe she's cultivating in us a deeper kind of attention.

4. SIGNATURE SUMMER FLAVORS

This week my older son, who lives in Japan, sent me a video of his preschool daughter, my only granddaughter, eating a wedge of watermelon. She was totally concentrating on bite after sweet bite and ate every bit of red all the way into the white of the rind. Then she asked for more. Watermelon is, for me, one of the signature flavors of summer. Another is my grandmother's homemade ice cream. We made it today to celebrate the Fourth of July. It's vanilla, but I can't say plain vanilla, because it has a secret ingredient: brown sugar. And it's amazing.

What is your signature summer flavor?

5. SUMMER AIR

A soft sea washed around the house,
A sea of summer air . . .
– Emily Dickinson –

The sky was a wonder today with mountains of clouds bunched and billowing, white edged with gray and gray edged with white, shouldering each other all the way across the horizon, some feathering at the edges as the upper currents frayed their puffed sides. Beyond them stretched an expanse of deepest sea blue. Take a minute to breathe deeply of the soft sea of summer air. Breathe out heaviness, breathe in buoyancy.

6. DAWDLE

The breeze at dawn has secrets to tell you.
Don't go back to sleep.
– Rumi –

When I think of the word *dawdle*, I think of the word *don't* as in don't dawdle. I can hear a parent or teacher saying that, hurrying children to come along. But children get distracted by the wonders of the world around them. They want to pause and look, touch, smell, and listen. They live in the present moment. Jesus famously said, "You must become like a child." I think he was talking about living in the present moment, seeing, touching, smelling, listening, tasting, wondering, appreciating the secrets of nature. So dawdle. Do.

7. A Steady Rain

I woke up to a steady rain this morning. Our back deck is now slick with rainwater reflecting the sky and trees above. Their reflection ripples as raindrops hit the puddles with small, white explosions. My dainty white windflowers are looking soggy. They've bowed to the rain as if they gave up trying to stand straight and have decided to nap the day away. The birdfeeder full of sunflower seeds has no takers this morning. I guess the birds are sheltering in place—except for two hummingbirds who don't seem bothered by the rain at all. They're zipping around their red-topped feeder, pausing for a drink, then flitting to a nearby branch. The raindrops that look small to me must make quite a splash for a hummingbird. But here they are, undaunted. And now that the rain is easing, the chickadees and finches are venturing out. Interesting that the ones showing up first are the small birds.

8. Not Sharing

Poet Pádraig Ó Tuama wrote, "[M]y love of poetry was a way of noticing, not just an art form." Do you have a way of noticing? Photography, sketching, painting, collaging, sculpting? Or writing, journaling—maybe only one or two words, a phrase, a poem, or entire pages of thoughts tumbling out? These are ways of lingering, and we often share the results. There's a beauty and openness and joy in sharing, but once in a while, it's okay not to share. In fact, occasionally, maybe often, it's best not to share. To eat a meal without posting a picture of it. To take a vacation without revealing your destination. To unlink with the world for a while. It's the lingering that's important, and the noticing. Sometimes the gift you notice is a treasure for you and only you. I have to remind myself that not all noticing needs to be documented or shared. Sometimes it's meant to be a secret, a treasured gift just for me.

9. PARTAKE

In those vernal seasons of the year,
when the air is calm and pleasant,
it were an injury and sullenness against Nature
not to go out and see her riches,
and partake
in her rejoicing with heaven and earth.
– John Milton –

Partake. It's a word I don't hear or use much. But it's a rich little word, a mashup of two words we use all the time: *part* and *take*. Like a puzzle, the words have been rearranged. They mean *take part*. If we "take part," we're "part takers." We partake. Or as we say more often, using a related word, we participate. In Milton's quote, he stretches out his hand and invites us to come along. *Partake*. It's an invitation.

10. The Wisdom of Orchids

My older son and his family gave me an orchid a few years ago. It seemed so exotic, I doubted that I could keep it alive. This spring it bloomed again with a lineup of white blossoms on two stems, an entire chorus line of orchids. Every time I looked at them, I almost expected them to burst into song. They've lasted for weeks, but the blooms are falling now, each one looking like the skirts of a dancer dropped on the floor after a performance. They leave behind a bare stem that will bloom again, I hope, after it gets some rest. That's the wisdom of these orchids, showing us that we need rest to bloom again.

11. Beetle Wings

> Ladybug, ladybug,
> fly away home.
> – Mother Goose –

My youngest grandson found a ladybug on the rim of a flower pot. She was so still, we thought she was dead, but when he picked her up, she crawled across his palm. Then with a flash of her wings, she flew. Actually, her flight was more like a hop with wings out. Ladybugs have a double pair of wings. Two hard, outer wings form the top of her body and protect two thin flight wings hidden underneath. To fly, she opens her outer wings and then unfolds her flight wings. It all happens so fast it's a blur. June bugs and other beetles do the same, and none of them fly very far. The next time you see a ladybug or other beetle, pause and look at its wings.

12. BALANCE

I paused to watch my grandson build a tower of small blocks today. He's always building something, and it's fascinating to watch him discover what works and what doesn't when he's stacking blocks or boxes or pillows or upside down flower pots. It's all a matter of balance. I can see that where he wants to add the next block won't work. Its weight will tip the structure over. But he doesn't want my instruction. And, really, he's learning the lesson better by trial and error. In pottery class, I had to learn how to center a lump of clay on the turning wheel before forming it into a vase or bowl or cup. Otherwise the piece was so unbalanced, it soon became unworkable. I did have instruction, but the real learning came by messing up several lumps of clay.

Balance is a good word for being centered. Centered indicates something stable that our life rotates around. The center is the fulcrum point on which our life is balanced. Look for things that are balanced or unbalanced today.

13. CLOUDY

> The mists above the morning rills
> Rise white as wings of prayer.
> – John Greenleaf Whittier –

My bird feeder is a brown-gray silhouette against the white-blue of an early morning, cloud-blanketed sky. In the space between the feeder and a leafy hackberry branch is the perfectly framed profile of a little finch. Now it flits off to be replaced by a chickadee. The grayed forms of this dusky morning are countered by bright golden ligularia blooming against the porch rail below. This variety of ligularia is called "midnight lady," which seems appropriate, because it's bright even on this dim day. I can imagine these blooms glowing in the depth of the night as they witness one day silently turning into another.

14. YOUR TREE

> Keep a green tree in your heart
> and perhaps the singing bird will come.
> – Chinese proverb –

What's happening with the tree you chose to follow through the seasons (see January 6)? How is it changing for summer? Or maybe the tree's not changing but its surroundings are.

15. GIFTS OF THE DAY

> May you live every day of your life.
> – Jonathan Swift –

St. Augustine once said, "I fear that Jesus will pass by me unnoticed." I fear that the gifts of this day will pass by me unnoticed—the cloud formations, the birds, the fragile blooms open to the sun at this moment, the peace within this day. So as I move through this day, I hope to look for the gifts that nature has for me and linger with them.

16. CREEPY CRAWLIES

There was a millipede in our basement today. I found him when I went to put clothes in the washer,

and I paused to watch him for a minute before I put him outside. He was fairly small as millipedes go, but he had all the little feet, and he was motoring right across the concrete floor. I wondered if he was hoping to reach an expanse of dirt sometime soon and dig in. I gave him a lift, a short flight to a better location. He curled into a little coil for the ride, but when I set him down on the ground outdoors, he stretched out and step-step-step-step-step-stepped on his way again.

17. ANGLES AND CORNERS

I lingered in bed for just a moment this morning, enjoying the angles and corners that shape my bedroom ceiling. Our house is older, and my bedroom is upstairs. The ceiling angles at the sides to match the roofline, then straightens toward the dormer windows, forming lots of angles and corners, which in turn create interesting shadows. The corners collect shadows so that where one wall meets another, the color changes, even though both walls are painted the same color of blue. One becomes a lighter shade, one becomes darker. Even those shades change with the angle and brightness of daylight shining through the windows.

Corners angle in or jut out. They can be curved and smooth or sharp and hard, shadowed in shelves, hidden in closets, small in tiny boxes, big at the end of a city block. Pause to notice a few corners today.

18. SIGNS OF SUMMER

There is much beauty here
because there is much beauty everywhere.
– Rainer Maria Rilke –

At the moment, what's your favorite sign of this summer season? I'm sitting outside enjoying the bees flitting from butterfly flowers to windflowers, which are one of my favorite signs of summer. Their delicate white blooms look like flying fairies as they bob in the breeze or under the weight of bees on their tall, thin stems. Whatever your favorite sign of summer is, linger with it for a moment.

19. NOSES

Some thirty inches from my nose
The frontier of my Person goes.
– W.H. Auden –

Auden seems to have been very precise about his personal space. Thirty inches. From his nose. It's possible that he was joking about his belly, but photographs don't show him looking particularly rotund, so I'm going with personal space. His nose was fairly prominent, large and rounded. Anyway, I'm noticing noses today, round, sharp, upturned, downturned, long and steep, short and shallow. And that's just on people. At the zoo last week, there were plenty of interesting noses on display: big and huffy on the Andean bear, tiny and rounded on the meerkats. Beaks and snouts, sniffers and diggers. Our zoo doesn't have elephants right now, but that would be a nose to notice.

20. FOOTSTEPS

My grandfather used to tell about how his father, my great-grandfather, built his own house. There were lots of children, so the second floor of the house was for them, while the first floor held the main bedroom, the kitchen, and the living room. Great-grandad intentionally built the stairs next to the wall of the main bedroom, where he could hear every groan and creak of the wooden steps. If any of the kids tried to sneak out at night, my great-grandfather would call out, "I hear ya'."

Listen for footsteps—the click-clack of heels, the pad-pad-pad of slippers, the rhythmic tap of a runner, the tick-tick of a dog prancing across the floor, or the creak of your own feet on the stairs.

21. MELTING SHADOWS

Tip of shadow,
rimmed in light,
your sharp edge softens
in the lowering sun

> and you melt
> into the quiet peace
> of night.
> – kh –

Notice how shadows change as the day passes.

22. VISITING BIRDS

> I believe that if one always looked at the skies,
> one would end up with wings.
> – Gustave Flaubert –

A brilliant yellow goldfinch, a rare visitor, flew down and perched on the rail of my back porch today but then left as fast as he had come, chased by the regulars at the feeder, the cardinals, chickadees, and titmice. In fact, the goldfinch dashed off so fast that he was just a flash of gold as he left.

Falcons and hawks visit our neighborhood from time to time. They usually land in trees nearby, although a couple of times, they've landed on the railing of our deck. But most often I see them flying high above. If I watch long enough, I can usually tell if it's a falcon or hawk, because the falcon is fast and rarely soars, while the hawk flaps a little and soars a lot, often in wide, slow circles. Sometimes in the evening, I see a dark, flapping figure cross the sky. The first few times I saw it, I wondered: Falcon? Hawk? But no, it was an entirely different creature: a bat.

23. DRIFTING

> Summer afternoon—summer afternoon;
> to me those have always been the two most beautiful
> words in the English language.
> – Henry James –

One of the joys of being in a swimming pool, for me, is not actually being in the pool but on the pool, drifting on a float, trailing a hand in the cool water, eyes closed to the brightness of the day, ears open to birds chirping and leaves rustling in the breeze. Drifting is a beautiful word. Drifts of bubbles, drifts of leaves, drifts of cherry blossoms tumbling from trees, drifting clouds, drifting hawks riding the currents high above. And my attention drifting away from details and drifting into the sky-wide embrace of a summer afternoon.

24. STORM

> Glorious the thunder's roar.
> – Christopher Smart –

I was raised in Texas with thunderhead clouds and rumbling summer storms. It was truly glorious to hear thunder grumble and growl from a big bellied sky or break through with a bullwhip crack and a flash of lightning. It was Nature's voice saying, "Heads-up!" I loved listening to a storm's distant, echoing approach, its overhead clash and boom, and its fading, rolling departure, the last growl of a spent storm. In my early twenties, I married and moved to Southern California, where thunderstorms were few and far between. We once had a mighty thunderstorm there, one to rival its Texas cousins. Traffic slowed. Pedestrians paused. People gawked at the sky. It was glorious.

25. TULIP POPLAR

> When a man plants a tree he plants himself.
> Every root is an anchor, over which he rests
> with grateful interest,
> and becomes sufficiently calm
> to feel the joy of living.
> – John Muir –

For Arbor Day in the spring of 1987, the year my older son was in second grade, his teacher sent each child home with a tree. Well, a twig, really. A potential tree. I let him choose where to plant it, and he decided on a spot in the center of the front yard. Fine with me. I didn't think it would grow anyway. It was just a stick, maybe six inches long. So he planted it, and it remained a scrawny stick until my husband ran over it with the mower, which shortened it considerably. Also fine with me. I didn't think it would grow anyway. But then it grew. Not by inches but by feet. It became a sapling with leaves that seemed too big for its girth. Looking at it was a little like looking at a puppy's big feet and knowing that this pup is going to be a large dog someday. Those leaves were a sign of things to come. My treasured tulip poplar is now a full-grown shade tree, taller than my two-story house. Yellow "tulips" with orange heart-shaped markings appear on it each spring. My husband mows around it.

26. Hot and Cold Running Water

> You never miss the water till the well runs dry.
> – early 17th century proverb –

I'm looking out my window through a screen drenched with rain, the drops clinging like little crystals to the webbing. Meanwhile, out west there's a drought and several fires. I wish I could send some of this rainwater west. We had a drought here several years ago, and I remember how a friend lost a whole stand of newly planted trees that just dried up.

I think I first learned to appreciate the water coming from my faucets when I was in college. My husband was in a band that was to play a gig in a small town in New Mexico, and I went with him. The band had several rooms reserved at a local hotel downtown, which looked like something out of an old Western movie. Painted on the front window was a sign that read, "Hot and Cold Running Water." Now this was in the 1970s, which might sound like a long time ago, but hot and cold running water had been a thing for a long time. Who wouldn't have hot and cold running water? The sign made me feel as if we'd been transported back in time to the early 1900s. I sometimes remember that sign when I turn on the water for my shower. I linger with the feel of hot and cold running water, and I'm grateful.

27. LINEN AND SKY

I bought a new air freshener called "Linen and Sky," and I'm in love with the fragrance. I don't know if it smells like linen—I have a linen shirt, which smells clean, but it doesn't smell like this air freshener. As far as sky, I've smelled lots of sky in my lifetime including the fresh smell of rain approaching, the chemical odor of smog in 1970s L.A., the stench of a meat-packing plant when the wind blew the wrong direction, the pungent stink of a paper mill, the acrid smell of fireworks, and the mouth-watering aroma of grill smoke and sizzling steak. The air freshener's "sky" fragrance obviously doesn't refer to any of these skies. The closest I can get to its scent is what I smell when viburnum is in bloom. I can happily breathe that sky. And the "sky" of this air freshener. It's a powdery fresh hug of a scent.

28. Tricks of Light

Our cat has started growling at her reflection when she passes a floor-length mirror in the hall or sees herself in the glass of the back door. I think she's decided another cat is encroaching on her territory. I guess reflections can fool you like that if you're a cat—and maybe even if you're a person. From indoors at night, the reflections in my glass back door show an exact replica of my kitchen that looks like it's on my deck. Two kitchens. I can easily imagine there's a parallel world just outside. The reflection took the indoors out. But reflections can also bring the outdoors in. At breakfast this morning, the surface of my coffee was a dark little pond reflecting an upside-down cameo of the trees outdoors. Indoors out. Outdoors in. Nature is playing tricks with light.

29. Detritus

I have a friend who sees beauty in the bits of nature that most of us pass by or trample over and sweep away: chips of dry fallen leaves, torn and faded petals, tiny feathers, bits of broken rock, mini-twigs—or simply detritus. I can hear her saying *detritus* with a gleam of passion in her eyes, a love for the detail most of us never even notice. Detritus. She sees beauty in it and draws its intricate patterns slowly, carefully, lovingly with the sharpest pencil lead and the finest-tipped pen. She's an artist.

A piece of detritus appeared in my kitchen window this morning, hanging between the glass and the screen. When I took a closer look, I saw that it was a leafy lacework a quarter-inch wide in the shape of a star. Its ragged, irregular outer edges framed an open center, a circle evenly trisected by miniscule spokes that made the tiny object look like a star-framed peace symbol. An almost invisible spider-silk held it in place, and it swayed slightly in the breeze. I got the sharpest pencil I could find and drew it.

30. THE POETRY OF THE EARTH

The poetry of the earth is never dead;
When all the birds are faint with the hot sun,

And hide in cooling trees, a voice will run
From hedge to hedge about the new-mown mead.
– John Keats –

When my youngest grandson was a toddler, he sometimes paused in the middle of play and looked up at me with eyes wide, eyebrows raised, and a hand cupped over one ear. That was his way of saying, "Did you hear that?" Maybe it was a chipmunk. A bird. The neighbor's dog. A jet overhead. Someone in the neighborhood hammering. Or mowing. Yes, I heard. Wasn't it amazing?

31. THE TOUCH OF A LEAF

My old, faithful African violet is blooming again. I took a closer look at it today, admired its pinkish purple cluster of blooms, and stroked the thick, wrinkled, fuzzy leaves. It's one of those plants that invites a touch.

I'm awed by how varied leaves are in their shapes and shades, in the patterns of their veins, in their texture, scent, and even flavor if they're edible, because many of them are. My purple shamrock's leaves are thin and delicate. My aloe plant is thick and prickly. The leaves of romaine in my refrigerator are crisp and wrinkly. Carrot tops are feathery. There's joy and wonder in the touch of a leaf.

AUGUST

1. NATURE BATHING

A few years ago, I began a practice of taking weekly walks at our local botanical gardens. I would hike the back trail, or rest silently in the pavilion of the Japanese Garden, or sit on a bench along one of the paths and sketch a tree or a stone bridge. Nature became a balm for me, a healing voice. Recently I read about a practice developed in Japan called *Shinrin-yoku*, which means "forest bathing." It's the practice of leaving outside cares behind and spending time in a woodland among the trees, absorbing the healing ambience of nature. I don't have a forest or woodland nearby, but I do have the botanical gardens. And I have my neighborhood. I have my own yard. It usually takes me only a moment to pause, breathe deeply, open my senses to the present, and feel nature's calming touch. It's not exactly forest bathing. Maybe it's nature bathing.

2. A LONG DRINK OF COOL WATER

I had pizza for lunch today, the everything-on-it kind. It was cheesy, peppery, tomato-tangy, and veggie juicy. Also salty. I've been thirsty ever since, and I'm noticing how refreshing and soothing a cool glass of water is. My grandson had only cheese on his pizza, but he's been thirsty too. He guzzled down a cup of water and said, "Ah!" It reminded me of hot summer days when I was only a bit older than he is now. My dad had brought home a huge tractor tire and laid it on its side in the back yard. My cousins and my little sister and I would sit on that tire with our legs in the hole as if we were sitting on a circular bench, and Mother would serve us ice-cold Kool-Aid. These days, I prefer plain water. There's nothing like a long drink of cool water on a hot day. Or after salty pizza

3. A CLOSER LOOK

> If your pictures aren't good enough,
> You aren't close enough.
> – Robert Capa –

In one of my large flower pots, zinnias are blooming in a variety of red, pink, orange, and yellow. Some of them have two rows of petals, which make a rather flat circle. Others are layered in a plump, mounded look that reminds me of a decorative pillow. All of them have yellow centers, which I thought were fairly ordinary until I looked closer. Then I saw that the centers looked like miniature circular gardens of tiny yellow flowers—flowers within a flower. Curious, I took a closer look at another favorite: dahlias. From a distance, my dahlia blooms have a yellow center encircled by a band of deep magenta that merges into a lighter pink at the ends of the petals. But when I looked closer, I saw that the sides of each petal curve up gently. They look like boats painted light at the outer end, gradually deepening to magenta on the inner end, which touches a yellow middle that looks like a collection of yellow candle flames. Miniature gardens, boats, candles—a close-up can be magical.

4. SHADE

Stands the Sun so close and mighty –
That our Minds are hot.
– Emily Dickinson –

The temperature has been in the 90s, and the sun has been relentless. Even plants that I watered yesterday look droopy now. My grandson and I venture out for a few minutes to put more sugar water in the hummingbird feeder. I'm wearing my gardening shoes, but he's barefoot—or has, as he likes to say, "naked feet"—so he hot-foots it across the sun-seared deck to the shade, where we lower the feeder and set about refilling it. It amazes me how, on a burning hot day like this, the shade provides enough relief that we can actually stand in it, while a few inches away, bare feet would burn. I'm grateful today for shade.

5. SKEINS, BEVIES, AND SHIMMERS

A flock of crows descended on our section of the neighborhood today. I have no idea why they chose us, but they flew in, perched in the trees, and cawed their greetings, which always sound cranky to me. A friend told me that a group of crows is called a murder. I looked it up, and she's right. They're called a murder because long ago, they signaled that an ambush was coming. I guess they rose as a flock at the approach of someone who had hoped to attack secretly.

I wondered, what about other birds? I discovered that a flock of finches is called a charm. Gulls are a colony. Larks are an exaltation. Sparrows are a host. Flying geese are called a skein. (I love that.) A flock of ducks is a team or a raft. Owls are a parliament. Wrens are a chime. Hummingbirds are also a chime or, my favorite, a shimmer. A group of robins is a blush. Cardinals are a college. Chickadees are a banditry, maybe because of their black "masks." Doves are a bevy. And another of my favorites: Cedar waxwings are an earful. Perfectly true in my experience.

6. SUMMER STORM

I stepped outdoors last night to watch lightning in the distance and was immediately engulfed in a sultry sauna of heavy air. It was too oppressive to linger, so I ducked back indoors. Moments later, the skies opened. It was a classic downpour. Rain falling in sheets. Lightning flashing. Thunder crackling. Water pooling in the streets. By this morning, the rain had moved east. But rainwater had weighed down the towering crape myrtle beside my back deck. Its clusters of curly, pink blossoms—some the size of a bunch of grapes, some as long as watermelons—had collected the rain. They had grown heavier and heavier until they bowed the branches down as far as the soaked soil in the poppy garden. But that had created a perfect archway over the redwood steps leading to my back deck. A raging storm had left us with a beautiful calm.

7. A QUICK PAUSE

> The reason why we have two ears
> and only one mouth
> Is that we may listen the more and talk the less.
> – Zeno of Citium –

I'm taking a quick pause to watch a clock with a second hand and note what I hear in sixty seconds. Ready, set . . . go. A lawnmower. The droning hum-buzz of an insect. A one-note call of a bird. A door slams in the distance. And that's it. A quick pause for listening.

8. PURPLES

I'm playing with purples today in a collage. It's a color I haven't used much in my art. But some of my favorite flowers are purple—lilacs, wisteria, irises, violets, pansies—so I'm daring to use it a bit more now. I think of it as a rich color. Maybe that's because I grew up drinking Welch's grape juice, which was kind of thick and had a dark, rich flavor. Plus purple has traditionally been the color for royalty and other rich people. I'll confess that I've made the common mistake of interchanging *purple* and *violet* in descriptions. But I've learned that purple is the name for the secondary color made by mixing red and blue, while violet is a bit bluer, closer to an amethyst color. Of course, there's more. There's plum and orchid and indigo (which is close to blue). There's mauve and wine and eggplant, periwinkle and fuchsia and mulberry. I could never point out all these shades and tints of purple in nature or in art, although I'm probably using all of them. Still, for today, the watchword is purple.

9. MAKING IT HOLY

> It is a beauteous evening, calm and free;
>   The holy time is quiet as a Nun
> Breathless with adoration; the broad sun
>   Is sinking down in his tranquility . . .
>   – William Wordsworth –

Evening, morning, afternoon, any time of day and any length of time, even a single minute, can be a holy time. We make it so by paying attention, by pausing in breathless adoration, by settling, if only for a moment, into tranquility.

10. ENTHUSIASTIC JOY

> Every day opens and closes like a flower,
>   noiseless, effortless.
> Divine peace glows on all the majestic landscape,

> like the silent enthusiastic joy that sometimes
> transfigures a noble human face.
> – John Muir –

"Silent enthusiastic joy." That's what I often see in a Thursday night art class. Music plays softly in the background as my friends and I work independently but side by side, each of us creating art that comes from our souls and nourishes our souls. It's then that I often notice in my friends' faces a "silent enthusiastic joy." But I picture other faces as well: my dad and sisters laughing uproariously in enthusiastic joy, delightfully not silent, and my friends in the church choir as we listen to our director with a silent enthusiasm that transforms into the joy of song. I'm claiming the thought of those faces of joy today, lingering with them for a moment or two and smiling to myself, noticing the joy and contentment they give me.

HEAVY, DROWSY DAYS

> Heavy is the green of the fields, heavy the trees
> With foliage hang, drowsy the hum of bees
> In the thund'rous air: the crowded scents lie low:
> Thro' tangle of weeds the river runs slow.
> – Robert Bridges –

I recently heard someone call this "high summer." Maybe like "high tide," summer is finding the outer edge of its reach and will now ebb back toward cooler weather. Writer Jeff Zentner calls this time of year "Hotumn." Other people call it "dog days," which I always thought referred to dogs slowing down because of the heat. Actually "dog days" refers to the brightest star in the constellation Canis Major, which means "big dog." Its brightest star is Sirius, which appears at sunrise from mid-July to mid-August, thus "dog days."

All of the labels above sound appropriate today. The whole week has been heavy, drowsy, sultry. Gardens hummed with bees and hummingbird wings. Lazy breezes drifted past full of fragrant scents from nodding blossoms. Then grumbling thunderstorms drenched it all until the sun broke through, stirring up the humidity again.

12. COMMON WEALTH

I recently read the word *commonwealth*. As I lingered with it for a moment, I realized I've often seen the word but never really thought about it: *common wealth,* the wealth we all have in common. It's all around us. I saw it this morning as I was taking out the trash: Two new balloon flowers, deep blue, had opened overnight. A red-orange rose had bloomed as well. I took a picture of each of them in the soft light of early morning, and now I'm thinking of my eyes as the lens of a camera. As I gaze straight ahead, I frame my shot, a panorama that extends outward side to side, up and down. I stand still and absorb this picture. What moves into the frame or out of the frame? What moves within the frame, and what is motionless in this moment? These riches of nature are free. They are our common wealth.

13. ROOTS

> Simplify the problem of life:
> distinguish the necessary and the real.
> Probe the earth to see
> where your main roots run.
> – Henry David Thoreau –

Cheekwood, the botanical gardens where I often walk, has some very old trees whose roots have emerged aboveground and wind around like mazes in the dirt near their trunks. On walks, I have to be careful not to stumble over them. Seeing them today made me curious about a tree rumor I had heard, so I did a bit of research. I had heard that a tree's roots spread down and out as far underground as their branches spread overhead, so I pictured a tree's root system as a mirror image of what I saw aboveground. I wondered if that was true. The answer: not really. According to the Harvard arboretum site, "It is not uncommon to find trees with root systems having an area with a diameter one, two, or more times the height of the tree . . . Roots grow where the resources of life are available."

I thought of our own lives and how we try to root ourselves in the nutrients our souls need not just to survive but to thrive. I think those people who seem to carry grace and calm within themselves, even when the whole world seems upset, have sunk a taproot into a deep soul-source of calm, a strength they consistently draw on to create strong roots that help them survive storms.

14. FORTUNE'S SPINDLE

In an 1813 letter, Lord Byron described his future wife, Annabella, who was an amateur mathematician. He wrote, "Her proceedings are quite rectangular." I am not remotely a mathematician, amateur or otherwise. My proceedings are wavy, even spiral at times. But I enjoy noticing rectangles. Rectangular panes in rectangular windows. Rectangular spaces between rails on the stairs. Rectangular steps. And in nature? Pure rectangles? The only thing I can think of is one of the strangest flowers I've ever seen, and it grows on a shrub beside our house. Each small flower has four creamy white rectangular petals extending out from a green center to form a cross. Within the green center there's a smaller cross of creamy white. The shrub is called Fortune's spindle, and I think the great fortune of spying its blooms is mine.

15. JUST BASKING

There's a medium-size finch sitting sideways on one of the perches at the bird feeder this morning. No other birds are around right now except for hummingbirds several feet away. The finch is so still, I'm beginning to wonder if she's all right. I once rescued a young finch who was caught between the cage bars of a different feeder. He had apparently tried to exit at the bottom, where the bars were closer together. One time I rescued a bird who had been trapped in a long thread that had wound around the branch of a bush. I wondered if she had chosen that thread to help build her nest, not knowing it was way too long to manage. For each rescue, I had put on gardening gloves, and I was about to get the gloves again for this finch when she hopped to a different perch, ate a bit, and then flew away. Maybe she had simply been enjoying the sunshine, just basking in the quiet of the morning.

16. TENDING

> Where you tend a rose, my lad,
> A thistle cannot grow.
> – Frances Hodgson Burnett –

Tend is short for *attend*, meaning *pay attention*. I definitely have a garden that needs tending right now. We've had lots of rain, and the weeds are growing like crazy, especially the vines that weave their way into the azalea bushes and climb the stems of lilies and cannas. French philosopher Simone Weil once said, "Attention is the rarest and purest form of generosity." I need to be more generous with my garden.

17. ON VACATION

> The only real voyage of discovery
> consists not in seeking new landscapes
> but in having new eyes.
> – Marcel Proust –

The lake is bright and calm today. I'm on vacation in Texas with extended family, staying at a house with a pool, a small, white-sand beach, and a boat. It's such a change of scenery that I'm noticing everything: colorful pink and yellow lantana blooms that look like a display of little bouquets; spiky palms; tall, feathery pampas grass; mesquites with scraggly twig limbs; and live oaks, compact and sturdy. Perched on the topmost leaves of this stand of live oaks is a dragonfly. I spy it only because it darts out as I'm looking up. As the dragonfly settles back onto its perch, I notice another dragonfly, motionless, silhouetted against the clear blue sky. Then I begin to see dragonflies everywhere perched atop the trees in silhouette, a whole swarm of them. Once in a while one flits out, then back. I assume they're catching tiny insects mid-air.

The view, the sounds, the scents are different here, out of the ordinary, so they catch my attention. Since I'm on vacation, it's easy to linger. Maybe I can return home with new eyes.

18. ABUNDANCE

Peaches are in season. Signs advertising Georgia peaches are popping up by local farmers' markets, where bins and boxes are full of produce: the fuzzy Georgia peaches, smooth green watermelons, fruity sweet cantaloupes with delicate tracery covering their skin, large heirloom tomatoes, plump squash, strawberries, onions, shiny heirloom tomatoes. My neighbor left a bag of tomatoes on our front porch last week, a gift from her garden. My own garden is overflowing with bell peppers—yellow, red, orange, and green. This is a season of abundance.

19. WHAT HAVE I MISSED?

> The eye is the best of artists.
> – Ralph Waldo Emerson –

I read that poet William Carlos Williams, like many writers, carried a notebook for jotting down his thoughts and observations. At the top of one page he wrote the heading, "Things I noticed today that I've missed until today." So with my eye as the artist, I'm hoping to notice something I've missed until now. I already see one thing: On the wall to the right of my desk is a charcoal gray scuff mark in the shape of a V as large as my palm. I don't know how long it's been there or how it got there. It's almost hidden by a shelf. My wall is a light sea blue. With my eye as an artist, it looks like a sea blue sky as a backdrop for a diving bird drawn in charcoal gray. It makes me wonder, what else have I missed?

20. LINGERING WITH WEARY

> I got the Weary Blues . . .
> – Langston Hughes –

I'm tired today. Weary. Paying attention to it. Lingering with it. Early to bed tonight.

Tired Nature's sweet restorer,
balmy sleep.
– Edward Young –

21. FIRST TO FALL

I counted twelve yellow leaves among the green in
the tulip poplar this morning. The elms are also
changing from dark green to yellow green, and the
first leaves are beginning to fall, although only one by
one, now and then, here and there, just enough for
the trees to let us know that while it's not autumn yet,
they know it's coming. They're getting a head start on the
occasion, determined not to be the last ones to the party.

22. A FULCRUM

Be like the Sun,
King without courtiers,
silent and still as a fulcrum.
– Rumi –

I'm wishing you a few moments of silence and
stillness today. Close your eyes. Listen to your breath.
Feel the subtle messages your skin receives from the
air and the textures you touch. Catch scents that drift
to you. Then open your eyes and focus on one small
object. Notice its shape, size, and colors. Listen to
your breath again. Feel the peace of the moment. You

are a fulcrum, a support, a point of balancing calm in the world.

23. WARM, BROODING DAYS

> The warm, brooding days are full of life
> and thoughts of life to come,
> ripening seeds with next summer in them
> or a hundred summers.
> – John Muir –

We have a second brood of wrens in our bluebird box this year. We cleaned out the box after wrens nested there in the spring. Recently, another pair took up residence. They spent a few days bringing in grass and building their nest. Now when the female flies in, a chorus of peeping greets her. I've seen one little hatchling peeking through the round door.

Brood as a verb has a double meaning, which I suspect was the way John Muir was using the word. For birds, it means to tend as a hen does when she sits on her eggs or keeps her young under her wings. But *brood* also means to ponder, to think deeply. So these warm days of summer are not only a time for birds to raise broods but also a time for us to brood, to think deeply about life. Our "thoughts of life to come," in Muir's words, hold next summer in them. Our thoughts hold a hundred summers. Our thoughts hold the future.

24. VARIETY

> Nature is not so poor as to possess
> only one of anything.
> – John Muir –

Nature echoes herself in abundance. All trees are similar, but each is different from the others, sometimes subtly, sometimes extravagantly. Flowers, birds, clouds, fish—all are themes and variations of beauty and wonder, gifts offered to us daily, ours simply for the noticing.

25. WHERE WE SIT

Edvard Munch, a Norwegian painter, said, "You should not paint the chair, but only what someone has felt about it." So I'm noticing how I feel when I sit in different places. I'm trying to imagine how I would paint the way I feel about my chair. Or chairs. I have several, so I'd have to make several paintings.

In my studio, I have a "back chair," notable because it has no back. I can sit there for a long time and my back is fine, but my shins get sore. I think I would paint that chair as two squares, flat, black, and overlapping at one corner. I also have a desk chair, where I'm sitting at present. It's a common, padded, office-type chair that swivels and rolls. Right now, I'm feeling a bit sore in my sit-bones, because I've been here a while. I would paint this chair as a sage-green U shape. Then there's my chair at the kitchen table, an upright with a straw seat to which I've added a pad because of the aforementioned sit-bones. I'd paint that chair as a checkerboard of cream color and wheat-gold. Last is my after-dinner chair, which gently rocks but isn't as comfortable as I'd hoped it would be. I'd paint it as a wavy squiggle of blue. I think I may be in the market for a new chair.

26. WONDERS TO HOLD AND KEEP

Behold the white wistarias –
The Milky Way blown by the wind.
– Hajin, translated by Asataro Miyamori –

Long ago, before *behold* meant *to gaze upon or observe*, it meant *hold* or *keep*. In a way, that's what we do when we observe something. Each season brings us wonders. We can hold on to them, keep them in our mind and heart so that, in turn, they can hold us and keep us in a place of calm and peace. Behold the candy-colored zinnias. Behold the fragrant citronella. Behold the cascade of crape myrtle blooms. Behold Nature's gifts.

27. A NECESSARY PAUSE

[Grasshopper] takes the lead
In summer luxury,—he has never done

With his delights; for when tired out with fun
He rests at ease beneath some pleasant weed.
                    – John Keats –

Grasshoppers, cicadas, droning bees drunk on nectar, these are lazy late-summer afternoon sounds. Not that I have much time to be lazy these days, but the buzzing of insects on branches overhead and in grasses underfoot reminds me of slower days in my childhood. It's not really that childhood afternoons spent outdoors in the West Texas heat could be called lazy, even if we were lolling about on a barely-moving swing or lying in the grass watching roly-poly bugs. No, those afternoons were a necessary pause, a child's rest and reverie, an expression of curiosity and wonder, a way of absorbing nature and beauty and goodness underscored by an orchestra of loud, raspy voices coming from tiny creatures in hedges and trees and grasses.

28. THE MUSIC OF TIME

In the 1600s, the artist Nicolas Poussin painted *A Dance to the Music of Time*, which featured the four seasons dancing to the sound of time. In the center of his painting, the personified seasons hold hands as they dance in a circle. To the left a baby sits on the ground playing a flute pipe, while to the right, an old man with wings sits on a stone playing a lute. At his side, another baby watches sand run through a small hourglass. In gray thunderclouds overhead, a chariot crosses the sky carrying a figure who holds a circle, probably the sun but maybe the moon. Obviously, time is passing.

It's a privilege to sit for a minute and listen to time pass. At this moment, I hear the ticking of a clock measuring time as the sun rises on a cool morning. Windflowers bob under the weight of a bee. A fat-jowled chipmunk scurries across the deck, pausing for a second to search for stray seeds. Two hummingbirds flit past twittering. A jay pipes up with a strident call. A cardinal lands on the rail of the deck, then flies away. A cricket chirrups in a rhythmic pulse. A dog barks from some yard west of us, echoed by a neighboring dog to the east. The bird feeder rattles as a nuthatch lands on it. I'm grateful for the privilege of hearing the music of time passing.

29. WISDOM OF THE CROSSROADS

Stop, look, and listen. That's what many of us were taught to do when we learned to drive. It's the wisdom of the crossroads. It's also the deepest call of our spirits, whispering to us: stop, look, and listen.

I live one block from a university that has a bell tower that chimes out the hour from eight in the morning to eight at night. To my mind, it's saying, heads-up; time is passing. It just chimed seven. I look out my bedroom window to see one of my elms silhouetted against an evening blue sky with patches of white clouds high enough to catch the last rays of the sun. Darker blue clouds line the lower horizon, already out of the sun's reach. A jet flies across with a deep-throated growl, red lights on its wing tips. Night-singing bugs are presenting an overture of this evening's musical featuring rasps, chirps, buzzes, and long droning whirrs. And now, in the time it has taken to write this, the white clouds have turned blue, and the overhead sky is deepening toward darkness. It's the twilight hour. Before the bell chimes eight, the sky will be dark.

30. FROM RUTS TO ADVENTURES

There was a warm sunset over the wooded valleys,
a yellowish tinge on the pines.
Reddish dun-coloured clouds
like dusky flames stood over it. . .
Before, I walked in the ruts of travel;
now I adventured.
– Henry David Thoreau –

A French saying commonly attributed to writer Jean-Baptiste Alphonse Karr says, "Some people are always grumbling because roses have thorns; I am grateful that thorns have roses." G.K. Chesterton made the same point in a different way: "An adventure is an inconvenience rightly considered. An inconvenience is an adventure wrongly considered." We can choose to see thorns or roses, inconveniences or adventures. We might as well choose roses and adventures. We might as well step out of the rut.

31. FORKS

I'm sitting at my laptop and pausing to look out the window, which I often do when I'm supposed to be thinking. And I am thinking, but I'm thinking about forks and noticing forks. Not the silverware kind but the kind where a tree trunk curves and branches out, and where branches divide so that one becomes two. I sketch the trees and notice that these forks are connection points. Flowers have them too, these dips or nodes where the main stem angles out to become a smaller stem with leaves and maybe blooms. I think of other forks like streams and rivers where one waterway branches into two. Or a road that divides, the kind that inspired Robert Frost to write, "The Road Not Taken." These connections, these points, these forks are places of change. I darken them a bit as I draw. My hand, my fingers, and my pencil "feel" them. They seem important.

Autumn

SEPTEMBER

1. SEEING THE MIRACULOUS

> The invariable mark of wisdom
> is to see the miraculous in the common.
> – Ralph Waldo Emerson –

This morning, there was dew on the white roses and the sunflower leaves and the cascades of creeping Jenny. I only noticed it because I bent down to smell a rose. It's been ages since I noticed dew. It's a common little miracle, appearing overnight and disappearing in full sunlight. I wonder how often I missed this little miracle by hurrying past.

Linger with something you pass every day, something common to you. Notice it with as many senses as you can. May you see the miraculous in the common.

2. THE BROWNING OF BLOOMS

The greenery in our landscape has yet to turn autumn brown, but it's headed that way. Some of our hydrangea blooms have already faded, but they tend to stay on their stems for weeks, creating an intriguing dried arrangement. I watch for these blossoms in their dry, brown state, because they're just as beautiful dry as they are in first bloom. The petals turn a translucent tan, and the veins in each petal show up as a fascinating web of darker brown. My hydrangea sits on the deck beyond a window, so I can watch it go through its seasonal changes. It was a Mother's Day gift from my older son a few years ago, and it continues to be a gift each day all year long.

3. ONE FALLEN LEAF

Adopt the pace of nature: her secret is patience.
– Ralph Waldo Emerson –

I found one fallen oak leaf on the sidewalk yesterday with a cracked acorn and a twig beside it, nature's art on display. It was a small foreshadowing of autumn. It will be weeks yet before all the leaves fall and the raking and mulching begin. Nature takes her time and gives us days to anticipate the cooler weather and the change in scenery. The anticipation is delicious.

Autumn is a tease of a season. Through green leaves, she peeks out here and there in a splash of yellow and a dash of orange before fully emerging in her grand red and gold. Leaves are beginning to drop a few at a time, but after a bit of patience, autumn will whisper a windy, "Shhh!" and they will shower down.

4. MYSTERY PLANT

A weed is no more than a flower in disguise,
Which is seen through at once, if love give a man
eyes.

– James Russell Lowell –

I pulled up my mystery weed today. A bird or
squirrel might have planted it. Or a seed may have
flown in on the wind. Or I might have planted it
myself along with the packet of mixed wildflower
seeds that I bought, not knowing what they would
turn out to be. I've figured out what most of them are.
Except for this mystery plant that grew up alongside
the others. At five feet tall, it's giving me a Jack-and-
the-Beanstalk vibe. It has more of a stalk than a stem
and stands thick and stiff and straight. It's growing like
. . . well, like a weed. About the time I thought it
would shoot up to the clouds, it formed small, candle-
shaped pods or "blooms" at the tops, making the plant
look like a candelabra. Then tufts of feathery fluff like
dandelion seeds peeked out from each "candle." Last
week I decided that was as far as I was going to go
with this plant, but before I could cut it down, I
noticed it was full of ants farming aphids. So I left it
for a few more days, because now I had an aphid

farm. Then we had a pounding rain, which bent the stalk in two, and that was its death knell. Out it came, candelabras, aphid farm, and all.

5. SOFT SOUNDS

Something told the wild geese
—It was time to go;
Though the fields lay golden
—Something whispered,—'Snow.'
Leaves were green and stirring,
—Berries luster-glossed,
But beneath warm feathers
—Something cautioned,—'Frost.'
– Rachel Field –

I've started a practice of trying to listen beyond or underneath the shouts and clangs and alerts and clashes that demand attention. I'm trying to rediscover soft sounds, the hums, the sighs, the whispers. It's like trying to pick out one instrument's musical line while listening to a symphony. Right now, under the birdsong and rasping call of the cicadas, there's a soft whispering whoosh. I think it's the sound of wind in the trees. It ebbs and flows and reminds me to listen for the constant, soft undertones of wonder, joy, peace, and hope in each day, the life-giving grace of love's whispers.

6. CRUNCHY, CREAMY, JUICY

As I put together a chef salad for supper tonight, I focused on noticing all the fresh ingredients and the color, texture, smell, and even sound as I sliced onions and celery, tore crisp wrinkly lettuce, and cracked and peeled boiled eggs. When I sat down to eat, I added flavor to the experience. Juicy red tomato. Slightly bitter, crunchy-clean celery. Root-sweet, bright orange carrots. Nutty, creamy, yellow-green avocado. Sharp green onion. Snappy home-grown bell pepper. Salty, grated, pale yellow parmesan. Tangy herb-flecked balsamic vinaigrette. I've been told that paying attention to food as we eat is part of what helps us feel satisfied and not overeat. I don't know if that's true or not. I just know it's a treat to notice each flavorful bite.

7. BUTTERFLIES

September is the month for Blue Morpho butterflies at Callaway Gardens in Georgia. My daughter-in-law and I took a girls' trip to Callaway in September a few years ago. The highlight of the trip was the butterfly center, a conservatory with glass walls and a high, glass-paned ceiling. The walkway inside wove us through a warm, humid, semi-tropical garden of trees, flowers, and butterflies. Some looked like brightly colored flying stained-glass windows, some had elegant black and white lattice designs, and some were tiger swallowtails with black tiger stripes gracing their yellow forewings. But the most unusual were the Blue Morphos with their rich blue wings narrowly outlined in black.

I noticed a butterfly today here at home, a yellow sulphur enjoying my crape myrtle blooms. I've seen a swallowtail and a viceroy as well. Usually they flit around the aptly named butterfly flowers or the lovely lavender-pink blooms called false dragonhead. They're "smelling" with their antennae and tasting with their feet, as I learned at Callaway Gardens. I also learned that a whole flock of butterflies is called a kaleidoscope. I can only imagine how amazing it would be to see a kaleidoscope of butterflies.

8. A BLESSING

Here's a blessing for you today:
A special breakfast for you today:
A plate of love,
A bowl of peace,
A spoon of kindness,
A fork of caring,
A glass of hope.
– based on a Vietnamese blessing –

9. SEEING SILVER

The last time our piano tuner came it was a cloudy, about-to-rain day. I welcomed him inside "on this gray day," as I put it. He laughed as he came in and told me that he had seen his elderly neighbor working in her garden. He had called to her, "How are you on this gray day?" She looked up, smiled, and said, "Oh, it's not a gray day. It's silver." I've heard overcast or rainy days described as gray or dark or dreary or gloomy but never silver. But silver is the way I'm going to see them from now on.

10. THE MATURE GARDEN

Seeds form,
full-bellied,
flat or beady,
hooked or teardrop.
Slowly, surely, steadily
they enfold life,
then calmly wait and rest
through dark days
and chill frost,
holding that life
snug and secure
for the time when they will

crack open to light
and life
and wonder.

- kh -

My young grandson, helping me prepare dinner, was fascinated with the secret that was hiding inside squash and bell pepper: seeds, flat and squashy in the squash, tiny and pebbly in the pepper. Who better than a preschooler to help me notice seeds? Well, maybe the squirrel who just strolled past my back door with a huge seed pod in her mouth. As I watch, she proceeds to bury it among my impatiens.

11. HOLD STILL

Hold still is a curious expression. Taken literally, it's a lovely image: holding stillness in our cupped hands, our thirsty hearts, our open minds; restfulness held like a treasure, quietly, carefully, gratefully. The dictionary definition of still is "free from turbulence or commotion." It's related to *stall* from the Greek *stellan*, which means to put or place. In that sense, it's akin to *settle*. When I'm training myself to pause, it helps to settle my body and try to coax my mind to *hold still* and stop pinging toward past and future concerns.

Cup your hands as if you're holding a bird. Close your eyes and *hold* stillness for a moment.

12. ITSIES

My mother died in autumn several years ago. A few years before she died, she told me that she had begun exercising—walking to be exact, walking through her house from room to room. Her house had a natural circuit: kitchen to hallway to living room, then back through the hall and into the kitchen again. She told me that as she walked, she looked at all her pictures and knick-knacks and thought about friends and family who had given her each one. Since she had many friends and a big family, she had a big collection. Over the years, she had been given decorative bowls and vases, figurines of birds and children, candlesticks, needlework pillows, porcelain thimbles, and coffee table books— "itsies," as one of my friends' grandmas calls those little dust-collectors that are important to us. I have itsies of my own. I've yet to tour my house to take stock of them, but once in a while, I suspect that someday I'll be lingering with them.

13. TO A TREE

Yours is not the way of words
or worried prayers.
When the warm wind whispers,
you dance.

When it wails and blows,
you bend.
You may lose a branch or two,
but when the storm has passed,
you stretch and brush the sky clean.
Sturdy and steady
like a magician,
you hold your limbs up to the sun
and blooms appear.
You birth your leaves,
and form your fruit,
and when the air grows cold
and the breeze bites,
you meet it standing tall.
You shiver yourself inward,
your leaves a glory of red and gold
before fading to a crisp brown.
You shed your seeds and leaves
and let the wind toss them up
and sweep them away in a skittery swirl.
And still you stand,
your long limbs a lacy pattern against the sky.
You were here before I prayed my first prayer.
You will be here after I pray my last.
By your simple presence, you calm my thoughts,
shush my agitation,
share the wisdom of the changing seasons.
But yours is not the way of words
or worried prayers.

No need.
You hold an ancient trust,
a sacred silence,
an inborn settledness,
a stillness of heart.
You are who you are.
You need no words.
You are the prayer.
- kh -

14. MAKE SOMETHING HAPPEN

On one of my walls, I have a plaque that says, "Be
still and know that I am." It's a Bible verse. God said,
"I am who I am." But that applies to us as well. I tell
myself to be still and know that I am. I exist. I'm here,
and that's good and right. But sometimes, I need to do
more than simply be still and know I exist. I need to
make something happen. I need to toss a pebble into
a pool, listen to the splash, and watch the ripples. I
need to blow a dandelion. I need to blow bubbles
with a straw in a glass of milk. I need to stir the milk
and watch the vortex. I need to create something, to
get my hands into paint or dig my fingers into dirt. I
need to dance. I need to notice me, not only to know
that I am but to be glad that I am. To celebrate that I
am.

15. LITTLE CREATURES

This morning, I noticed ants crawling into my house from around the windowsill above my kitchen sink. Sugar ants were not really what I wanted to notice today, but there they are, a battalion of them, checking out the grout between the tiles of the backsplash, parading toward the counter. We've had some heavy rain lately, so they may have been flooded out of their home in the ground. As I clean them away, I notice a spider between the window pane and the screen. A small spider with a big belly. She has spun silky threads along the pane and attached them to the screen. I can only see the web where the morning sun glints off its threads. I lean closer and notice that the spider has caught something and has it immobile near her. It's an ant. A sugar ant. She's helping me clean up. I think she's in for a feast.

16. LOOKING FOR POETRY

> There is not a particle of life
> which does not bear poetry within it.
> – Gustave Flaubert –

What calls to me today? What stirs an emotional echo in me? Always, it's trees. Always, it's the sky. But what else? Today it's the rooftops I see from the window above my desk, the angles of one repeated in the other, the triangled dormers above double windows, the way the shadows lie across them. Look for the poetry, the emotional echo, in an object, a place, or an event today. "We all write poems," said novelist John Fowles. "It is simply that poets are the ones who write in words."

17. GRASS HEADS

When I was a child, my friends and I would pluck prickly seed heads of grass, place one on our forearm, and then move our fist back and forth, flexing our muscles, which made the grass heads crawl up our arm like a caterpillar. I've tried it recently with the grass that grows in my yard, but I have yet to make it work the way it did when I was young. Maybe it's a different kind of grass. Or maybe my memory has made the "crawling" more real than it was. Even when I was a child, the seed head didn't crawl far before it fell off. But it was magical to us. We were making caterpillars out of seed grass.

Linger a moment if you see grass with seed heads on it today. It may be growing in a park or enjoying the freedom of an empty lot. You may see entire fields of grass—oats, barley, wheat. You may see decorative grasses in pots in front of buildings or in displays in windows or in landscaping in a neighbor's yard. Maybe you'll find grass that has gone to seed emerging from cracks in a sidewalk. Maybe the seed heads are small and prickly. Maybe you can pluck one, place it on your forearm, flex your muscles, and watch it crawl like a caterpillar.

18. BIRDS IN THE HEART

If you want to see birds,
you must have birds in your heart.
– John Burroughs –

The temperature dipped last night, so this morning is cool, and a variety of birds have turned out to welcome it. I see the regulars: house finches, wrens, chickadees, titmice, and cardinals. But today we have a surprise visitor, a dove, who perches on the vacant bluebird house for a minute before moving on. Then there's the "watchbird," a wren who hangs around and always chatters a warning when our cat enters the scene. His warning sounds like a playing card attached to the spokes on a bike's tires, like kids used to do when I was growing up.

Now I'm thinking about what John Burroughs said about seeing birds. I'm thinking that it applies to more than just birds. Maybe to see kindness, we must have kindness in our hearts. To see beauty, our hearts must hold beauty. To see peace, our hearts must hold peace.

19. THE LAST HURRAH

It's a silver day, warm and humid with a cool edge. Clouds are low, blanketing the sky. Most trees are still lush and green but with a yellowish cast to them, while a few are getting a head start on turning gold and red. Bees are busy among the windflowers. As they land, the thin stems dip. When they take off, the stems bob back up and the white blooms dance. Now that the weather is no longer baking hot, lots of flowers are perking up. My coral bells are full of tiny pink blooms on coral stems. The dahlia also has new blooms, although they're smaller than they were in early summer. New marigold blooms are emerging. Even the hydrangea has new leaves. And my chrysanthemum buds are plump, ready to open any day now. I'm soaking up this feeling of being under a leafy canopy, the last hurrah of summer, full and lush and abundant.

20. HARVEST MOON

> The whole moon and the entire sky
> are reflected in dewdrops on the grass,
> or even in one drop of water.
> – Dogen Kigen –

September's full moon is called the Harvest Moon. It rises at dusk, so for a couple of days around the time of the Harvest Moon, evenings are bright. The same thing happens in October, but it's called the Hunter's Moon. I try to remember to watch these full moons as they rise, because that's when they appear huge and golden-orange. Even if I forget to watch for moonrise, I still see the full moon when I wake during the night. I see its reflection in the phone I've set out to recharge and in the glass of water I left on my desk. As I look out the window, the full moon peeks in. Sometimes it looks as if it's snagged in the branches of a tree. Sometimes the tree looks like it's cradling the moon in its arms. And as I look at the Harvest Moon, I have the feeling that it sees its reflection in my eyes.

21. AUTUMN RAIN

> How beautiful the leaves grow old.
> How full of light and color are their last days.
> – John Burroughs –

These are the last days for leaves that are not evergreens like Southern magnolias are. While these grand old ladies keep their thick, shiny green leaves, the maples turn red, the tulip poplars go bright yellow, and the dogwoods turn rust-red and coral. Each leaf of the crape myrtle looks tie-dyed in varying tints of red, orange, yellow, and green. When the next chilly autumn rain falls, leaves will come tumbling down with it. And if the rain brings wind, even the grand old Southern magnolia will lose a few leaves.

22. Sounds of Autumn

Listen . . .
With faint dry sound,
Like steps of passing ghosts,
The leaves, frost-crisp'd, break from the trees
And fall.
– Adelaide Crapsey –

Take a moment to still your soul, to linger and listen to the sounds of this season.

23. Changing the Dance

When the music changes,
so does the dance.
– Africa proverb –

As seasons change, it's as if Nature changes her music. Warm-weather birds migrate, owls move closer in, insects go silent, and the wind whines a bit. Even the train's call in the distance sounds louder and lonelier. Maybe it's time to change our own dance, to swing, sway, and stomp. Make it wild or wistful. Make it wondrous or wishful. Make it fully yours as I make it fully mine, keeping time with the music of this season of our lives, letting our music and our dance come from the depths of our heart, letting it sing of goodness and grace, love and hope.

24. WEATHER FORECASTER

Life starts all over again
When it gets crisp in the fall.
– F. Scott Fitzgerald –

Birds are unusually busy this evening. A cardinal, a nuthatch, two chickadees, a titmouse, two hummingbirds, and even a goldfinch are not in their usual take-your-time mood. No perching on the crook that holds the feeder, no dawdling beside the birdbath. Just quick and to the point, snatch a seed and fly. Maybe they sense a change of air pressure. Maybe they feel a cold edge on the breeze telling them that rain is expected this evening, bringing a cold front. Some of them will fly south soon. I hear a flock of geese honking as they pass. Nature is their weather forecaster, telling them it's time.

25. AUTUMN WIND

The shifting wind
swirls with stories –
a girl's kite plucked high,
a beachcomber's hair ruffled,
a gardener's hat tossed to the rose bush,
a cafe awning dismantled,
a dog's nose kissed,
secret stories
shared with the wind.
"Here's a hint,"
it whispers,
brushing past
chilled with frost,
laden with rain,
woven with wood smoke.
Hush. Hush.
Listen. Listen.
It's your story too.
– kh –

Feel the wind. Listen as it tiptoes past in a whisper, or waltzes with swaying branches, or twirls like an ice skater scattering sparkles of frost in wild abandon. Watch. Listen. Feel the wind.

26. VOICES

I've been thinking of my friend Karen's voice, maybe because I'm on the fundraising team at Art & Soul, and we just had an online auction and sale of her artwork and supplies, which she donated to us before she died. This weekend, I worked at the studio, where I set out her supplies for sale: paper and paint, pencils and canvases, empty notebooks. I bought some for myself. Her amazing collages and paintings were on display as well, and as I stood there admiring them, I could hear in my mind her soft southern drawl and her bouncy laugh. She was truly a good friend. I remember walking into the studio for a class a couple of years ago, and almost everyone was there already, including Karen. They were gathered around a table in the back. I paused for a minute listening to their voices. I can still hear them, each one with a different timbre, a unique cadence and lilt. I had to smile. They are all beautiful. I treasure those voices.

If you could step into a room and hear the voices that you love most, the voices that encourage you and make you smile, whose voices would you hear?

27. TWILIGHT

The trees are ruffle-edged swathes of black silhouetted against a twilight of powdery gray-blue that is deepening fast. I sit indoors, windows open, listening to a chorus of chirping night bugs, some on a continuous pedal tone while the trill of others swells and fades over and over again. As twilight darkens, the windows I'm looking through become a mirror of the brightest images in the room where I sit. A thin streak of bright white light under the cabinet spotlights an arrangement of five sunflowers in vivid yellow, the images doubled because of the double-paned windows. That's all I can see now as the twilight darkens into full night. But the insect chorus continues. A dog barks, and a screech owl repeats its wavering call ending in a soft murmured coo.

28. AUTUMN SHADOW-WATCHING

The sun is reaching its southern angle for the season, making autumn a good time for shadow-watching. I was with my toddler grandson one fall when he discovered his shadow. We were visiting our local botanical gardens, and as we strolled down the sidewalk, our elongated shadows strolled ahead of us. We paused in the middle of the sidewalk and waved at our shadows. Our shadows waved back. Standing there with a toddler, I was struck once again by the wonder of shadows. You can't catch one or hold it in your hand. It's there, yet it's not a thing; it's a silent, visual echo. Its presence is caused by absence—the absence of light. Yet that absence is caused by a presence—something that blocks the light. And a shadow doesn't appear unless there's light somewhere. That's my grown-up wonder. A toddler's wonder is the simple delight of discovering shadows.

29. ROUND

Round is the sound
of a deep-throated owl.
Round is arms
encircling a child.
Round is a raindrop,
a song-filled cathedral,
or ripples on water
around a tossed pebble.
Round is a tunnel,
the rumble of thunder,
the puff of a breath,
and eyes wide with wonder.
– kh –

Autumn feels to me like a round season, plump and full, maybe because of the roundness of pumpkins and squash, apples and berries, pies and cookies, even in the O's in *goodness* and the round, warm sound of the word *home*. Or maybe the round feeling of the season comes from sensing time circling around, headed toward rounding out the months that will end one year and begin the next, completing a cycle, a circle, a round.

30. FALL LEAVES

Look how the crape myrtle leaves glow
on the first chilly morning of early autumn.
Sunrays slide across outstretched limbs
and pause on top to pool on the leaves
in a sparkling white veil of light.

Look how the sun turns poplar leaves into golden
flags that dip and shiver in the breeze.
Soon they'll let go and flutter down
and make an autumn carpet,
leaving a lace of bare branches overhead.

But for now, the leaves are white veils
and golden flames,
the glory of a season ending,
the hope of a season to come.
– kh –

OCTOBER

1. FRUITFULNESS

Give me October's meditative haze,
Its gossamer mornings, dewy-wimpled eves…
And all is peace, peace, and plump fruitfulness.
– Alfred Austin –

I'm holding an apple in one hand, feeling its weight, its rounded shape, its slightly bumpy texture. It's red, fading to yellow on one side. A gala. I cut into it crosswise to see the star at its center, which looks more like a flower to me. Some of the brown seeds fall out. The flesh is creamy yellow and crunchy with a slightly sweet, slightly tart flavor. Just right. Peace. Peace and plump fruitfulness.

2. OCTOBER WIND

Already it is October,
and the wind blows strong to the sea
from the hills where snow must have fallen,
the wind is polished with snow.
–D.H. Lawrence –

At last cooler weather has settled in. I fill my lungs with air that carries the scent of wood smoke. A cold, sharp, snow-polished breeze gusts now and then with a rush and whirl that shakes loose the shivering gold and red leaves and whispers, "Welcome. Welcome to October."

3. NATURE'S AUTUMN ART

What is autumn? . . .
A second spring, where every leaf is a flower.
– Albert Camus –

Nature is a designer, an artist, a painter, a composer. She waltzes through neighborhoods and city blocks in the middle of the night arranging leaves, twigs, and seeds in patterns on sidewalks, in driveways, and on porch steps, maybe a trio of bamboo leaves on top of moss; or a stem of dark red leaves alongside a fan of pine straw; or an oak leaf, a twig, an acorn, and a ruffle of lichen. She leaves us these gifts each night for free. Most of them are gone by the end of the day, blown by the wind or scattered by squirrels or chipmunks or our own footsteps. But no matter. The Artist will visit again tonight.

LIKE SMOKE ACROSS THE SKY

In the cloud-gray mornings
I heard the herons flying;
And when I came into my garden,
My silken outer-garment
Trailed over withered leaves.
A dry leaf crumbles at a touch,
But I have seen many Autumns
With herons blowing like smoke
Across the sky.
– Amy Lowell–

I have a flock of geese. I don't mean they're mine exactly. And I don't mean a large gaggle either. I mean seven geese flying low over my yard every morning. I hear them before I see them. Crawnk-crawnking, they announce their flight, and I look up and search the sky. Here they come, seven in a V. Sometimes they fly past to the south of my yard, but today they flew straight overhead and low, wings pumping. And I was happy.

5. SQUINTING

When I was a child, I often squinted at lights to make them split into starbursts, as I expect most children do. Squinting was especially fun at night riding in a car, because night lights are so distinct and colorful. I could angle my head this way and that and make the starbursts shift and wink. Sometimes I still squint at lights. This morning, I squinted at the view outside the window above my desk, which turned the view into an impressionist painting. Swathes of light angled across patches of dark. There were greens and yellows, a splash of red, the curving brown of a tree trunk, and plops of tan where a rooftop showed through. Autumn is a rich tapestry of color.

Try the impressionist's view. Squint or unfocus your eyes. Pick out lights and darks, colors and hues. Make night lights burst into stars.

6. PAUSES OF SILENCE

Moments of silence are part of the music.
- Anonymous –

When I was learning to read music in junior high (called middle school these days) the choir teacher taught us to clap when we saw a note and pause, counting the beats, when we saw a rest sign. I remember that it felt like the end of the world if I clapped on a rest when everyone else was pausing. I'm in a church choir now and would still feel mortified if I sang when everyone else was silent. But I smile thinking of the musical symbols we call rests. We're not so much resting as thinking about holding that pause for the exact time it calls for and preparing to hit the right note when we come back in.

In music, pauses create rhythm and interest and meaning. It's not so different in life. If you listen to music, or even birdsong, listen to the pauses. Feel the space between the notes. Then think of your life as a unique composition, a musical score. Where are the pauses? As pianist and composer Artur Schnabel says, "that is where the art resides."

7. UNDERFOOT

Look underfoot.
You are always nearer
to the true sources of your power
than you think.
The lure of the distant and the difficult is deceptive.
The great opportunity is where you are.

Don't despise your own place and hour.
Every place is the center of the world.
– John Burroughs –

I'm trying to pay attention to what's underfoot in this season—the crunch of fallen leaves, the shape of stepping stones, the puddles left from a night of rain. The seeds that have scattered from the hackberries. And the rabbit that scampered off as I stepped outside. He wasn't underfoot exactly, but he could have been. We were that close. But he moved so fast that my best view of him was his puffed white tail.

8. SMALL CRAWLERS

> Nature is to be found in her entirety
> nowhere more than in her smallest creatures.
> – Pliny the Elder –

I think of October as spider month outdoors. The funnel web spiders are spinning their tunnel webs in the front windows again. At some point, I'll clean the webs off the windows, but these spiders are fascinating to watch, keeping out of sight behind the shutters and darting out through their funnels when a hapless insect ventures in. Those webs, I don't mind too much. It's the huge, traditional-looking webs of the large orb spiders that make me shiver. Orb spiders are harmless, but several times, I've unwittingly walked through their webs. One web stretched across our front door. One spanned the top of the stairs on our deck. That will teach me to slow down and look before I step.

Needless to say, I'm noticing webs this month. But they're worth lingering with—if you're not bumping into them. Especially if you can catch sight of a spider as she's spinning. It's a fascinating process and an amazing structure. She's one of Nature's artists.

9. GOLD

> The beauty that shimmers
> in the yellow afternoons of October,
> who ever could clutch it?
> – Ralph Waldo Emerson –

If you're searching for gold, you may be in luck. This is the season. Take time to enjoy nature's gold wherever you find it this week.

> Autumn dresses up in gold,
> the richest season of the soul.
> – unknown –

10. FINGERPRINTS AND BOWLS

Today I had a bowl of chicken enchilada soup for lunch in a bowl I made in a pottery course in college. It has been years since I used any bowl from the set I made. Still, it seemed to be the exact thing I needed to go with the soup. It's an earthy-looking piece of pottery, glazed with a creamy tan color speckled with dark brown. The underside of the bowl is rough where

I cut it off the wheel and has my pre-marriage initials carved into it. But my favorite part is the print of my own fingers that form a whorled pattern beginning at the inside center of the bowl and moving in wider circles as the bowl gets wider. In fact, that describes the process as well. Kicking the wheel as the clay turned in the center, I inserted my thumbs and gently pulled the clay wider, pressing my fingers where I wanted the clay to thin. Finger marks on pottery have always fascinated me, because they're unique to the potter. I'm a bit awed studying this bowl almost half a century later, seeing the trail of my young adult finger marks, sensing the hopes and dreams they left in the clay.

Hold a bowl for a moment and feel its lightness or its weight. What is it made of? What color is it? Is it smooth, round, square, textured? Linger with it.

THE CENTER OF THINGS

> The nature of God is a circle
> of which the center is everywhere
> and the circumference is nowhere.
> – Empedocles –

A round, prickly pillow of yellow sits at the center of my red chrysanthemums. The coreopsis has reverse colors: petals of yellow holding a center of red that looks painted on; you can see where the imaginary paintbrush swooped up the petal with red paint and then stopped. It's like a landing strip for bees. The centers of my white mandevillas are so yellow, they look as if they've swallowed sunlight.

The center of a flower. The center of a pattern on a plate. The center of a backyard. The center of a kitchen. With some things, it's easy to locate the center. It's not as easy with others. I'm focusing on the center of things today. But maybe, as Empedocles said, the center is everywhere.

12. Noticing "Enough"

> Enough is as good as a feast.
> – 14th century proverb –

It takes some practice to notice enough and linger there. Maybe in some cases, it takes a lifetime of practice, like paying attention to what I'm eating and how fast I'm eating so that I'm aware of my stomach saying, "Enough." Otherwise, I mindlessly reach for more. Where is enough when I'm buying holiday gifts? Where is enough when I'm working on a project? Where is enough when I'm trying to keep up, but my body is tiring? Or when my mind is weary? Or when my emotions are frayed? Where is enough when it comes to writing this entry? Okay, that's getting meta, but I'm leaning toward agreeing with myself: It takes a lifetime of practice.

13. FROM HERE TO THERE

When I first moved to Nashville about forty years ago, I had to concentrate on my route to go anywhere. North on Belmont, left on Glen Echo, left on Hillsboro, right on Abbott-Martin. The supermarket is on the left. I would look for landmarks, too. The post office, the high school, the pharmacy, the Exxon station. Then one day, I found myself pulling into the parking lot of the supermarket without even remembering how I got there. I was no longer consciously paying attention to street names or landmarks. My thoughts were elsewhere. So my challenge today is to focus on the present moment of moving from here to there instead of letting my mind wander.

If you go somewhere today, pay attention to the details of how you get from here to there and what you see along the way. Linger in the present moment of moving from one place to another. Moving around is really a marvel when you think about it.

14. MID-OCTOBER GARDEN

The cannas are still in full bloom, red ones, yellow ones, and some yellow, spotted with red as if a painter took a paintbrush and flicked red paint at them. Clusters of nandina berries, which have been green, are starting to blush pink on one side. By winter, they'll be fully red. The Virginia creeper vine has turned rusty red, and squirrels are scampering around with large seeds and nuts looking for a place to stash them. The garden is moving toward its final act for this season. There will be a new grand opening in the spring, a reprise of Nature's beloved classic, but maybe debuting a few new stars.

15. SPENDING TIME

Spend time seems to be a good way to describe what I do every day. I don't often linger with that idea, but I spent yesterday with my preschool grandson. We went to the grocery store, played games, had lunch, read books, and built a house with couch cushions. But we also spent money yesterday when we went to the grocery store. We spent it on bread and onions and squash and spinach and chicken and cookies. Spending money yesterday was my choice. Spending time was not. My time gets spent each day with or without my intentions.

How we spend our time really comes down to this very moment we're living in. We only have right now. The present. And the present is always rolling forward to become, well, the present. Which leads me to another interesting phrase: Take your time. Take it. Take it in hand. Take it to heart. Take the present moment, linger in it, notice it, live it with all your senses. Spend it well.

16. STACKS

As I wait for my grandson to arrive today, I'm looking at a stack of blocks. I left it standing after his last visit, because it's an intricate stack of large cardboard blocks in primary colors, and my grandson tucked plastic dinosaurs and insects strategically in nooks between the blocks. On top, he stacked a board that creates a tabletop on which he placed plastic space ships and more insects, a red plastic snake, and a miniature tea kettle. Quite the stack.

Now I'm noticing stacks of all kinds. A stack of games in boxes. A stack of toy bins. A stack of paper and paints. A stack of white pottery bowls in the cupboard, one inside the other. A stack of books, one atop the other. A neighbor's stack of gray, smooth stones, a cairn with the largest stone at the bottom, the smallest at the top. Today, it seems, is for noticing stacks.

17. WORDS

> We have to unlearn hurrying.
> – Robin Wall Kimmerer –

When I see a quote that hums in my heart or sparks my spirit, I write it down. Sometimes I linger with a quote and meditate by repeating it slowly several times, emphasizing a different word each time. Last night, I wrote down the Robin Wall Kimmerer quote. It's the one I'm meditating on today:

"We have to unlearn hurrying."

We have to unlearn hurrying—not just me but all of us.

We *have to* unlearn hurrying—it's necessary, not optional if we want to live a whole, healthy life.

We have to *unlearn* hurrying—ah, we've learned something we need to unlearn, to set aside, to reverse, to change direction and go the other way. Learning takes time. Unlearning may take time as well.

We have to unlearn *hurrying*—to slow down, to pause, to linger.

"We have to unlearn hurrying."

18. SPLENDID SUN

> Give me the splendid silent sun,
> with all his beams full-dazzling;

Give me juicy autumnal fruit, ripe
and red from the orchard;
Give me a field where the
unmow'd grass grows;
Give me an arbor, give me the trellis'd grape;
Give me fresh corn and wheat—give me
serene-moving animals, teaching content.
– Walt Whitman –

Linger with the splendid, silent sun as it changes
angles in this season.

19. A WINDOW INTO AUTUMN

Autumn from my window
is all green-gold
sparkling in sunlight,
leaf-on-leaf shadow and
wind-waving branches.
Or cloud-grayed into muted colors,
dimmed and whispering,
full moon shrouded by mist,
umbra-swept and owl-kept
and frosted by midnight.

Autumn from my window
breezes in, chill and crisp,
laced with smoke scent and leaf-drift,
late blooms and seed-rich pods.
The year is full and ripe and hearty

with the round bounty of the season,
ready to fill us to the brim with warm thoughts
to carry us through the coming cold
and buoy us across winter waves
into the rich new rise of spring.
– kh –

What does autumn look like from your window? Linger at the window you chose to use as a frame (see January 19). How has the scene changed from summer? As a reminder: If your view is a nature scene, let it be a sacred space, a small revelation of nature. If your view is a building or other structure, let it be a small tribute to shapes, textures, and shadows. Either way, it's a unique view just for you.

20. A CLEAR DAY

I heard the sweet lark sing
in the clear air of the day.
– Samuel Ferguson –

Today is clear and crisp-cool and cloudless. The maples are dark berry red against the deep blue of the sky. In ancient times, people who spoke Latin might have described this weather as serenus, which means "clear, cloudless, untroubled." That's where we get our word serene. I'm lingering a moment with the serenity of this day.

21. IN THE PALM OF MY HAND

As I drank my coffee this morning, I spied a smooth, round, white rock sitting beside a flower pot on my deck. Had it been there long? If so, why hadn't I noticed it before? I went outside and picked it up. It's really not white but a cream color. And it's really not smooth but rough. And it's really not round except on the side that was facing me when I first saw it. It's a bit dirty. Nothing to treasure unless you're a four-year-old boy. Maybe that's where it came from. It fits perfectly in the palm of my hand, and I close my fist around it. It feels good. Solid. Warm. I think I was wrong about whose treasure it is. It's mine.

22. CREEPING CUCUMBER

I'm lingering in my garden this morning, noticing how tall the mahonia has grown with its shiny, dark green leaves with prickly edges—like holly leaves only larger. On the ground is a pine cone. I see another. And another. They're prickly, too, so I'm thinking that today is for noticing prickly things. Then I see that a vine has wound its way around the fence along the side yard. It's daintier than ivy and has green, oval berries that look like miniature watermelons. So what is this vine? I have a new app that identifies plants, so I look it up and discover that it's creeping cucumber. Sounds kind of spooky. I can imagine it in a spooky story, overgrowing anything in its path. It's easy to pull up. But what if it comes back again? What if it multiplies? I can picture a whole haunted house overgrown by creeping cucumber.

23. REACHING

Our cat often reaches for the doorknob when she wants to go out. It's a sleek reach, an elegant reach, a simple stretch of her feline body. I think of my sons when they were small reaching up to be carried, which makes me think of my grandsons reaching up to be carried. My youngest grandson is almost too heavy to carry now, but how can I resist that reach?

The flowers in my garden reach for the sun. Vines reach up when they have something to climb. Fountains reach up as far as they can before the water splashes back down. The creeping Jenny in the flower box on my back porch reaches not up but down like a waterfall of green. The weeping redbud next door reaches down as well.

And now I'm noticing my own reach. To change a lightbulb. To retrieve a book from the top shelf. To touch the floor when I'm exercising. I reach dozens of times a day and have never lingered with the feel of it before. Now I'm amazed at how marvelous it is to be able to stretch out my arms and reach. Especially when I'm reaching down to pick up my grandson.

24. PUMPKIN PATCH

Pumpkins have been piled high for weeks at farmers' markets and at the local botanical gardens. Besides the traditional orange-all-over, they come in orange with green stripes, white with orange stripes, red-orange, and believe-it-or-not pink. Some are even purplish with red splotches as if an artist accidentally flicked paint their way. And they're all sizes, shapes, and textures, too. Some are so large that I can imagine them becoming a princess's coach, at least for a child princess. Some are tall and oval, some are traditionally round, and others are squatty as if they were squashed. Which, in a sense, they are—squash, I mean. There's something satisfying about holding a pumpkin, feeling the roundness, the fullness, the heft. Here's this thing that's ripe and full. Ripe and full as life itself.

25. NOTICING IN REVERSE

Sometimes, I want to go through a day in a foggy blur noticing no details and, instead, settle into a quiet reverie, fogged in, restfully ignoring the world around me. Since I've done so many things by habit for so many years, I can semi-sleepwalk through a day, or at least through parts of it. And sometimes that's okay with me. But the older I get, the more precious time becomes, and I want to minimize those foggy, blurry days. I want to be awake and aware, to be present for life, to practice lingering and noticing. In order to unfog and nudge myself to notice, I sometimes do something in reverse order if it's possible, something like cleaning the bathroom. I usually start with the sink, move to the tub, then the mirror, the toilet, and the floor. I usually water plants on my deck starting with the plants by the rail, finishing with the pots by the house. It's simple to reverse the order. When I do, I see my deck garden from a different perspective. If I reverse the order, I have to think. I have to be present and notice. Maybe I should get into bed on the right instead of the left. Or put my shirt on before my pants. I guess I could even write this book starting at the end instead of the beginning. What would I notice?

26. YOUR TREE

The forest will answer you in the way you call to it.
– Finnish proverb –

What's happening with the tree you chose to follow through the seasons (see January 6)? How is it changing? Or maybe the tree's not changing but its surroundings are.

27. TREE BARK

With gentle hand
touch—for there is a spirit in the woods.
– William Wordsworth –

Even though zoos showcase animals (and the Nashville zoo is wonderful for that), our zoo also has interesting plants. Last week at the zoo, I was drawn to a tree with an unusual pattern of bark mottled in splotches of rough gray against smooth, leathery, reddish tan. The top layer seemed to be peeling back, revealing another layer underneath. It was as if the tree was molting. Fortunately, it was labeled: a lacebark elm.

Seeing the lacebark reminded me of the bark on other trees, mostly those in my own yard. There's the smooth bark of the Japanese maple and the bumpy gray bark of our grandfatherly hackberry. Our tulip poplar has a thick, grayish, ridged bark. In the far corners of our backyard are American elms with bark that is deeply furrowed and coarse. Between the elms stands a row of longleaf pine with orange-brown, scaly trunks. And beside our porch, there's a crape myrtle with a bone-smooth, patched trunk that reminds me of the lacebark.

There's such beauty and wonder in the patterns and textures all around us, just quietly there, waiting for us to notice.

28. TINY POINT, VAST UNIVERSE

Each tree and leaf and star show how
the universe is part of this one cry,
that every life is noted and is cherished,

and nothing loved is ever lost or perished.
– Madeleine L'Engle –

A speaker at church today told about traveling to Kansas, where the land is mostly flat and the sky is big. He was awed by the feeling of "being one small point in a vast space." I knew exactly what he meant. I've felt that way myself driving across West Texas. Or standing on a beach by the Pacific Ocean and watching a rainstorm blow in from the horizon. Or looking out over miles of mountain ridges from a high point in the Colorado Rockies. Or gazing up into a moonless, star-filled sky in my own back yard. It's good for me to pull my head out of the details of the day and feel my smallness, to linger with it for a moment, to wonder at the expanse of the world around me and the vastness of the universe. It's good to breathe it into my lungs, to carry it with me in my heart.

29. MOON ECHOES

Earlier today, I looked at a picture of the cycles of the moon to find out (again) which direction it waxes and wanes. I was reminded that when the fingernail moon is a right-hand crescent with "horns" pointed left, it's waxing. When it's a left-hand crescent with "horns" pointed right, it's waning. The line-up of moon photographs that showed the order of these stages reminded me of ellipses. I like to think of them that way. "I may wane," they say, "but I'll be back . . ."

Even as the moon wanes, it's as if she has flung echoes of her full-moon self into the world, tucking away small reflections of her shape here and there. Circles show up in droplets of rain, in growth rings on a tree stump, in mushroom tops, in a bird puffed up in cold weather. Something about circles echoing the full moon is warmly satisfying to me. "Wholeness is our deepest need," we sang in a hymn at church last Sunday. Maybe that's why the full moon warms me— it's a symbol of wholeness.

30. SACRED SPACES

Everybody needs beauty as well as bread,
places to play in and pray in,
where nature may heal
and give strength to body and soul.
Between every two pines
is a doorway to a new world.
– John Muir –

Sacred. Dedicated to the divine. Worthy of respect and reverence. Holy. Or maybe wholly, since it's akin to the Old English word for whole. That's what I'm feeling as I sit with reverence in my yard in the shade of towering trees and feel the breeze and listen to a choir of birds. This is the most sacred of places, an echo of sacred places all over the world on mountaintops and in valleys, at seashores and beside lakes, under the canopy of the woods or under the tent of the wide sky. Some indoor spaces seem sacred to me as well: the art studio, the sanctuary at church, my own bed. Viewed from another angle, I can see that in some way, we carry the sacred in our hearts so that whatever our location, our presence makes it sacred. Still, if I had to choose one sacred spot, I'd come back to nature, where "between every two pines" or elms or lilies or rosebushes "is a doorway to a new world."

31. CAT WEATHER

> Ink-black cat purrs like
> knuckles rubbing a washboard
> rattling a rib cage.
> – kh –

These cool, crisp mornings are what we at our house call "cat weather." These are not the lazy hot days when our cat shambles across the deck and plops down in a shady spot to loll about all day. No, these are days when our cat, like every cat we've had, literally gallops through the house, tail fluffed, heading for the back door, eager to get outside. She must have seen a squirrel or a rabbit or a chipmunk. Or another cat, because after all, this is cat weather when cats suddenly seem to acquire an energy they shelved during warmer months. Maybe their instincts tell them this is good hunting weather.

Last week, I spied our cat crouching as still as stone on the back deck. Earlier, I had spilled sunflower seeds while refilling the birdfeeder. Now, a chipmunk was stuffing those seeds in his already-full cheeks. The chipmunk was only inches away from the cat but seemed oblivious to her presence. I knew that within seconds, the cat would pounce, so I headed for the door. The chipmunk scampered. The cat seemed to sigh. She sat up. Winnie the Pooh's voice came to mind from when he'd been foiled from taking forbidden honey: "I wasn't going to *eat* it; I was just going to *taste* it."

How would you describe today's weather?

NOVEMBER

1. AN AUTUMN SCENT

> Trees are made of air primarily.
> When they are burned, they go back to air,
> and in the flaming heat
> is released the flaming heat of the sun
> which was bound in to convert the air into tree.
> – Richard Feynman –

Feynman was a theoretical physicist, but his description of burning trees sounds almost mystical. Born with the help of the sun's energy, a tree gives that energy as it burns. I thought of that last night as

I smelled the smoke from a neighbor's fireplace. It was a pleasant scent to linger with, a warm, soft, brown-gray scent, the scent of autumn. I also thought of autumns when I was a child. The local college a few blocks away from our house had Homecoming in mid-autumn. As part of the festivities, the students would build a huge, towering pile of wood. The night before their big football game, they would have a pep rally and burn the wood in a magnificent bonfire. My family would always drive to the campus and watch it.

Notice a scent today and linger with it. What scent reminds you of autumn?

2. PENCIL TO PAPER

A friend just gave me a new set of pencils. I've been sketching with one of them, and I'm making a point of noticing how the pencil feels as an extension of my hand. I like lingering with the tactile sense of sketching as well as the soft swish of the pencil, now fast, now slow, as it passes over the paper, leaving its mark. I switch now to a pen, one that my friends recommended, a "really nice" pen. The feel is different from the pencil but pleasant. It's louder as it sketches.

It's interesting to pay attention to the sensations of tools that are an extension of my hand: scissors, hairbrush, screwdriver, fork and spoon and knife, paintbrush, needle and thread. There's sight, sound, and texture involved. Fork, spoon, and knife are associated with scent and flavor. Pay attention to the tools you use today, to how they feel in your hand. Notice how they partner with you.

3. UNCONTAINED BEAUTY

I am the lover of uncontained and immortal beauty.
– Ralph Waldo Emerson –

Uncontained. That describes the seeds of my milkweed butterfly flowers. Their finger-long, oval seed pods, which were still connected to the stem, had broken open. Inside, toward the stem end, were stacks of small, flat, oval, copper-colored seeds. Each seed had what looked like a stream of white hair coming out of one end. But at the top of the pod, a couple of seeds that had partially pulled loose were in the reverse position: The seeds were on top, and the white "hair" was fanned out like a dancer's skirt. The setting sun glinted off their thin, white hair-like filaments. I think these beautiful little dancers were waiting for the wind to whisk them up and away so they could plant themselves in a new location and grow, flower, seed and reseed uncontained and immortal beauty.

4. DUSK

Let thy west wind sleep on
The lake; speak silence with thy glimmering eyes,

> And wash the dusk with silver.
> – William Blake –

So much of nature speaks in silence, and it's most often when we're silent that we hear it. Ours is a noisy world. If the sky is clear enough, notice stars as they appear at dusk. Linger with them as dusk becomes twilight and then darkness. Watch stars spangle the night sky.

5. GARNERING

> That man is happiest
> who lives from day to day
> and asks no more,
> garnering the simple goodness of life.
> – Euripides –

For the last two years, I've grown ornamental peppers. When they're at the peak of their growth, the peppers—red, orange, and yellow—look like candle flames among the green leaves. This year, I decided that since ornamental peppers grew well for me, bell peppers would probably grow well too. As a bonus, they'd be edible. I was right. They grew and grew and grew—red, orange, yellow, purple, and green. I garner a few each week to use in sauces and salads.

I've always thought of the word *garner* as a synonym for *gather*. But I discovered that there's actually a bit more to it. *Garner* comes from the Latin word for *grain* and means not just "to gather" but "to gather into storage." So I'm garnering peppers, because I have more than we can eat. I'm going to dice them and store them in the freezer. At the rate they're growing, I may never have to buy a bell pepper again.

Notice the simple goodness of life this week. Garner it. Gather it and store it within your spirit.

6. COLD WEATHER TEXTURE

I'm lingering a moment with the thick, soft texture of my sweater, running my fingers over the ribbing of my corduroy pants, and feeling the comfort of warm, soft socks. One of my daughters-in-law is from Norway. Her mother knits intricate Nordic patterns into socks and mittens and sweaters and caps. In Norway, sweater weather has already been around for weeks, but here, we're just now digging into our closets for warm weather clothes. Now that the air is nippy, it's a pleasure to snuggle into sweaters, sweat shirts, jackets, flannels, and thicker socks. I'm also pulling out my trusty, oversize, yellow bed-sweater. I knitted it when I was sixteen and now wear it to bed as an extra layer on cold nights. When I was sixteen, I would never have dreamed that I'd still be wearing it over fifty years later. I couldn't even imagine a me of fifty years later! And yet, here I am in my old, oversized, yellow sweater.

7. The Scent of Cooking Food

Surprise dinners. That's what my mother called evening meals that she slow-cooked in the oven. She would spread out one large sheet of foil for each person. On top, she'd layer slices of vegetables, any that she had on hand but usually squash, carrots, and yellow onion. The top layer was a slice of meat, usually pork chop, but it could be a hamburger patty or a chicken breast. She would then wrap the foil of each person's meal around the veggies and meat to make a closed packet, which she'd bake for three hours in the oven. I do the same now, pouring my favorite marinade on top before closing the packet. It's not a surprise to me what's inside, but when I was growing up, you never knew exactly what you'd find when you opened it. One of the amazing things about this dinner, though, is the buttery, peppery aroma as it's baking. If I'm upstairs and come down, the scent meets me on the way. If I'm outside and come in, like I did yesterday as Surprise Dinners were cooking, the smell makes my mouth water and my stomach growl. The scent of cooking food inspires lingering.

8. On the Schedule

Every five weeks on my calendar is a scheduled bit of lingering and one I gladly pay for: a haircut. My hair is very short, but one of my great pleasures is getting it trimmed. And one of the pleasures of getting it trimmed is the shampoo and scalp massage that come first. Getting a haircut is one of those experiences that is so relaxing and sense-filled—the fragrance, the feel, the sound of water and sudsing and snips and hair drying—that it's perfect for lingering in the moment. It's also one of those experiences that becomes familiar the more you do it, and I sometimes find myself, as I did yesterday, leaving the salon realizing that I didn't fully sink into the moment. Focusing on the senses for a minute or two renews me, and I had let that opportunity slip. Still, it's on the calendar for five weeks from now. I hope to be more mindful next time. Meanwhile, I'll enjoy the feel of combing my short hair.

9. GRAY

> Shadow is a colour as light is,
> but less brilliant;
> light and shadow are only the relation
> of two tones.
> – Paul Cezanne –

Today I took a painting class and spent part of the time working out hues and values of shadows, which are not usually gray or black but contain color. As the amazing watercolor artist Yuko Nagayama wrote, "[T]here are surely colors that exist within darkness and shadow." So this week, I'm noticing shadows everywhere, big and small, spiked and curved, indoors and out. I'm trying to linger long enough to spy the colors that surely exist within them.

10. HANDS

> The narrowest hinge in my hand
> puts to scorn all machinery.
> – Walt Whitman –

I remember holding my granny's hand when I was a child, studying its brown age spots freckled across the soft, baggy skin, which I could gently pinch into hills. Her fingernails were thick and filed into clean ovals. They were working hands, the hands of a gardener. My hands are a lot like hers now, graced with brown age spots. The hills on my hands are veins that run like blue-gray roads across freckled maps. My fingernails are not like hers; they have always been thin and breakable. I keep them trimmed short, which makes me less concerned about getting them broken or dirty when I'm gardening or painting. At the moment, I'm typing away at the keyboard, noticing how my hands look, how they move, how it feels to tap the keys, how if I think about which letters to type, I slow down. If I just let these fingers go, they fly, the narrowest hinges putting to scorn the machinery.

11. MORE GEESE

This morning about 7:30 I heard geese approaching. I looked to the sky and waited for them as the morning air drifted in, cooling my arms. A jet passed high, flying east. Then the geese appeared from the southwest over the trees, flying northeast. I expected to see the usual seven geese, but this was a whole squadron flying in, their long necks leading their bodies, their wings gently waving as they pulsed across the still, cloudy sky. As their honking faded, the hushed world settled back into soft chirps and tweets and the whispery rush of cars in the distance. My morning was richer for their visit.

12. NOISE

> Go placidly amid the noise.
> – Max Ehrmann –

My grandson loves to push the button on the coffee grinder, and we let him do it with supervision. But it is loud. And it is grinding. And that's a big part of why he loves it. With the coffee grinder, he can make a monstrous noise without getting shushed. It's not a bad thing to linger with noise. The lawn mower is noisy. The leaf blower. The trash truck. They crash in and make me notice. How can I not? But, as it turns out, I have the capacity not to notice even the noises if they're familiar enough. I hear the trash truck rumbling down the street, and I simply turn my attention elsewhere. Today, I had to ask, "Did the trash truck come? I didn't hear it."

13. WINDOW SHADES

Sunshine is delicious.
– John Ruskin –

As our part of the earth angles away from the sun, its bright beams shoot straight and hot through my south windows. I've had to start lowering the shades when I work at my desk or I find myself squinting and considering sunscreen. It's a seasonal occurrence, this lowering of the shades. By choice, I have no curtains. I prefer no shades either. I like open windows everywhere. But then there's the matter of privacy for our neighbors and for us. Also, there's the sun. So as I lower these shades, I'm lingering with the soft zipping sound. I run a finger down the ridged white fabric that zigzags in and out, copied by a second layer that creates a honeycomb visible from the side. Straight on, they look gently striped, alternating between a white gray at each sloped upper zig and a soft gray shadow at each sloped lower zag. The shades are translucent, too, which means soft shadows of nearby trees show through. When the sun hits full on, the shadows are sharper, and the shades take on a gold tint. Ah, that sun, that painter, that colorist. Sunshine is delicious.

14. WITNESS

> Witnessing has always felt like sacred work to me.
> – Jennie Nash –

Jennie Nash is a book coach who mentors writers and trains book coaches. When she talks about witnessing, she means witnessing the growth of writers as they create their books. At Art & Soul Nashville, we have a practice of witnessing at the end of our classes and creative sessions. It's not a critique. It's a look at what each of us has created and telling how each piece of art makes us feel. What does it remind me of? What does it say to me? It may strike each of us differently. It's not a matter of right or wrong, of good or bad. Each person's artwork is valid. In witnessing, we're connecting with the piece and the artist and seeing, feeling, maybe touching, maybe hearing, using our hearts to receive it as a gift. We're holding it as a valued creation. It's sacred work.

It's the same with the world around us. In seeing and hearing, touching, tasting, smelling, feeling, we're connecting with nature and with the way humans interact with nature. We're holding it as a valued creation. We're witnessing. It's sacred work.

15. LIGHTS IN THE DARK

It's night time now, and I'm looking out an upstairs window into the darkness. I see four lights lined up almost vertically. The lowest is on the side of our neighbor's garage. It's distinct, bright white with a yellow cast. Over the garage in the yard behind our neighbor is a white light with an orange tint glowing like a starburst between trees. I happen to know that it's from the back window of a house one street over. Above and to the left of the starburst is a light that's round and golden-yellow: the street light on that block. Above that is a bright white light: the half-moon. These four lights remind me of a connect-the-dots activity. Mentally, I do connect these dots, creating an imaginary arrow that runs from the bottom up through the moon and keeps going straight out into the stars.

16. SPIRALS

Several years ago, our neighbors replaced the traditional outdoor stairs to their second-floor apartment with a black iron spiral staircase. I was excited, because that's the view I have from my kitchen window when I'm at the sink, and a spiral staircase is much more interesting than a traditional straight one. But what I like best about the spiral

staircase is its shadow. The handrail shadows are
large curves, while the spindle shadows flow straight
down over the red orange bricks of the upper wall of
the house, then curve as they cross the uneven, gray
stone of the lower wall. The shadows of the triangular
stair treads look like the flattened blades of a
windmill. The lines of the staircase itself cross all
those shadows to make a fascinating in-and-out,
swerve-and-spiral picture.

So I'm noticing spirals today. Rotini pasta. A spiral
tendril on a vine outdoors. Steam rising in a gentle
spiral from a cup of hot coffee. A spiral notebook
that's casting its own loopy shadow. It's a fascinating,
inviting shape, the spiral.

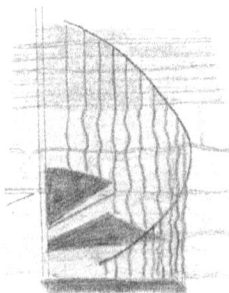

17. THE SCENT OF HOME

I have been here before,
But when or how I cannot tell:

> I know the grass beyond the door,
> The sweet keen smell,
> The sighing sound, the lights around the shore.
> – Dante Gabriel Rossetti –

Last night, I lit a new candle made of coconut wax. It's now unlit, but I have it beside me, and I'm lingering with its fragrance, "Moso Bamboo." It's a soft, clean, broad scent with a warm fruity edge. It makes me think of pillows. Now I'm wondering if I could describe the smell of my house before I had the candle. So many scents go into the accumulated aroma that greets me when I walk in. The house of my childhood smelled like a mix of new and old fabric with a hint of plastic and floor wax. I remember being uncomfortable going to other peoples' houses, because those places had a different smell. My in-laws' house in Georgia held a dank, earthy smell mingled with the scent of pines. But I can't narrow down a smell for my own house. I guess it's a mix of books and paint and paper with a hint of damp basement and whatever's cooking. And now Moso Bamboo. What does my house smell like? It smells like—well, like home.

18. A Scene Change

> Willows whiten, aspens quiver,
> Little breezes dusk and shiver.
> – Alfred, Lord Tennyson –

When you step out your door today, notice how the scene has changed from summer. What's different about what you see and smell and hear and feel in the air? Each day opens its palm and offer us gifts of the season. Linger with it. Catch its scent. Taste its flavors. Hear its song. Pay attention to this day. Tomorrow's gifts will be different.

19. BREATH OF GOD

> I talk of branches dancing in the wind
> but what I mean is the breath of God.
>
> – Rumi –

Last night the wind went wild, scratching tree branches against the siding of my house and rattling the window screens. Now the wind has settled to a breeze, and the dance of the branches has become a slow ballet. What is the dance like in your part of the world?

20. EVERYDAY TREASURES

In a cabinet in my sunroom is a box full of random toys. Yellow ping pong balls. A red whistle that looks like a bird. A Jacob's ladder. A set of felt beanbags in primary colors. Miniature bowling pins and a ball that doesn't look like it came with the set. A yoyo. And other odds and ends of playthings. Yesterday, my youngest grandson found a marble in that box. Just a single marble. But it's blue, his favorite color. It became the favored toy and rated an escape from the box into the outside world. My grandson has gone home, but the blue marble now sits on a shelf in my sunroom. I roll it between my palms, feel the small, hard, smooth globe. I eye it and see the way it catches and reflects the glint of light from a window. I roll it and hear the soft rattle across the wood floor.

Open a catch-all box or junk drawer and rummage around. Pay attention to the textures you touch. What's the smallest thing in the drawer? What's the largest? To a child, some of these things might seem like treasure. With the heart of a child, choose your treasure from this drawer and help it make its escape.

21. A NEW FLAVOR

At the grocery store, I occasionally buy a wedge of cheese in a new flavor. As I was pondering the choices at the cheese counter this week, a woman passing by paused and said, "If you're up for something adventurous, try the lemon Wensleydale." Indeed, I was feeling adventurous, so I bought it. And it was truly amazing, a bit sweet, a bit tart with lemon zest. It was a linger-awhile, melt-in-the-mouth dessert cheese.

Taste something you've never tried before. A strange fruit. A vegetable you usually bypass. A new type of bread. Or a different kind of cheese. Maybe the lemon Wensleydale.

22. LISTEN TO THE EDGE

In David Whyte's poem "Setting Out at Dusk," he mentions "small sounds at the edge of silence." Most of the summer insects have gone silent by this time of year. The one sound at the edge of dusky silence is the call of an owl. Sometimes it's the deep hoo-hoot of the great horned owl or maybe the barred owl. Sometimes it's the quivery descending whistle of the screech owl. But here in the city, there are other soft sounds at the edge of silence. The almost-not-there sounds. A jet passing high above and disappearing in the distance. The slam of a car door on the next block. The heater turning on. A whoosh or peep or tick of something so quiet that it's unidentifiable. Listen to the small sounds. Linger at the edge of silence.

23. DOTS

Bold black dots on white tissue paper caught my attention today. The paper had been wrapped around a gift given to me by an artist friend who loves the art of Yayoi. Yayoi Kusama is a wonderfully colorful artist who is known for painting polka dots as a motif. My friend chose that paper with love. And now I'm noticing dots. Small tan dots on soft, sage green sections of a quilt. Small balls of crape myrtle seeds that look like two-dimensional dots silhouetted against the deep blue of the sky. Pinpoints of stars in a picture of the heavens, dots flung across outer space. Freckles on my own arm. Pepper sprinkled on my salad. Keep your eyes open for dots today.

24. JOY

> Joy is found in gratitude,
> gratitude is found in awareness,
> awareness is found in pausing
> and paying grace-full attention
> to life.
> – kh –

Right now, life sounds pretty loud to me. A yard service is mowing next door. They come every couple of weeks with two riding mowers. As the mowers zip down the driveway to the back yard, I feel the vibration through the floor. Sound growls out of them with two sustained notes: a low throaty roar and a high whine. They work fast. Now comes a trimmer buzzing as if it's harnessed a whole choir of bees. The sounds fade as they move to the other side of the house. Then out comes the leaf blower with a raspy start and stop, a whoosh and a guttural grumble. And then they're done. How quiet the afternoon sounds now. I am grateful. And joyful.

25. SIGNS OF THE SEASON

> This is one of the still, hushed, ripe days
> when we fancy we might hear
> the beating of Nature's heart.
> – John Muir –

At the moment, what's your favorite sign of the season? Find it and linger in it. Listen for the beating of Nature's heart.

26. ARCHES

The garden supply catalogue that I like is advertising arch trellises. I sigh with wishes. I don't know where I would put an arch like that. Arches, especially tall ones, seem to be frames for what's ahead, invitations to explore, doorways into what's beyond. I can't think of a place in my yard that I could put an arch where there would be a beyond. Still, an arch strikes me as an elegant shape. Doors and windows and trellises that arch seem restful, inviting, comforting. So now I'm noticing arches all around: the spout on a watering can, a faucet, eyebrows. Arching branches seem protective like an umbrella. Arches are elegant. But I think I like arches most because of their gentleness, smoothness, and openness. An arch is a friendly, peaceful, hopeful shape.

27. THE WONDER OF SMALL GIFTS

This day is a gift—
the breeze brushing my face,
the call of the chickadee,
the glint of sunrise on the windowpane,
the flavor of nut-warm coffee
and morning blueberries,
the wonder of breath,
one and then another,
receiving the moment,
the day,
the grace,
the gift.
– kh –

In the wonder of this holiday season of bright bows and shiny paper, may we also find wonder in the small, common gifts that grace every day.

28. INDOOR LIGHTS

Darkness came before the night.
– Margaret Wise Brown –

Each classroom of the elementary school I attended had one wall made entirely of windows. On most days, the sun was bright and we didn't need the overhead lights.

But on rainy days, which could get quite dark, the room lights had to be on. I always felt a sense of wonder walking into the room when the lights were on. It felt protective as if we were cocooned. And it was exciting. It was dark in the daytime, and the lights were on in the schoolroom!

Now, in our part of the time zone at this time of year, dusk comes early and deepens to darkness before people get home from work. Lights come on in stores and office buildings and neighborhood houses, and I feel that wonder again.

29. TAPPING ON THE ROOF

Cedar waxwings rise
like clouds from gnarled branches
stripped now of berries.
– kh –

One late autumn morning a few years ago, I awoke to the sound of tap-tap-taps overhead on my roof, accompanied by a constant high, thin, pulsing squeal, like someone was trying to play the highest note on the thinnest of violin strings. I looked out the window and discovered that a huge flock of cedar waxwings had landed in the hackberry trees and were joyfully feasting on the berries. Stray berries were dropping on the roof, tap-tap-tapping like small hailstones. The waxwings' call was the high, thin sound I was hearing, what one bird book refers to as "high-pitched, hissy whistled notes."

Look and listen for birds today. How would you describe their call?

30. WILTED BEAUTY

> The last red-gold leaves
> flutter like prayer flags
> in the chill breeze.
> They are holding on.
> And so am I.
> – kh –

Much of my garden has turned brown and brittle. Petals and leaves that remain on their stems are dry now. Seed pods have fallen or hang empty. The ligularia, whose splitting seed pod looked like a Dr. Seuss creature with a spray of tan hair, has now gone bald. But there's beauty here in nature's dried arrangements. The hydrangea petals are a favorite of mine. In their dry form, they hang on long after other blooms have dropped. The petals are tan and paper-thin, veined in brown. Basil is fascinating as well with tiny, crisp, ruff-like ledges stacked in a line up and down its stems. Then there are pine cones, hard and prickly, dark brown tipped with tan. The world is brown and brittle and beautiful.

> The death of flowers in this garden
> is only change from one form of beauty
> to another.
> – John Muir –

DECEMBER

1. WISDOM AND WONDER

Wisdom begins in wonder.
– Socrates –

My favorite definition for *wonder* is *excited amazed admiration*. And for *wisdom: the ability to discern inner qualities*. So to read Socrates with a fresh view: "Wisdom begins in wonder" means "the ability to discern inner qualities begins in excited amazed admiration." I'm lingering with wisdom and wonder today. I'm noticing where I find excited amazed admiration. Breathe out weariness, breathe in awe.

May this season be full of wonder and wisdom for you.

2. MOON IN THE MORNING

Like the moon,
you will sometimes be a crescent
and sometimes full.
– Rumi –

There is a half-moon in the clear blue morning sky overhead and a bit to the west. As I look up, a breeze freshens and ruffles the evergreens. There's something magical about seeing the moon in the daytime.

3. SQUARES

Squares are solid little figures,
as wide as they are tall,
four corners just the same,
no curving, none at all.

A square will take no nonsense.
It's all business, precise turns.
Its squatty body solid stance
makes cubes and blocks stand firm.

They're in windowpanes and postage stamps,
in boxes and in lids.
In chocolate and crackers, they make s'mores,
and that's just what I did.

– kh –

A dear friend gave me an origami kit for my birthday. Each figure starts with a square and ends up as a boat or a flower or a box. That reminded me to show my grandson how to make paper snowflakes from a square of white paper the way we used to do in elementary school art class. So today, I'm making paper snowflakes and lingering with the idea of squares, looking for them, and thinking of how to describe them. Of course, in honor of squares, I had to get out square graham crackers, put a square of chocolate on top, and make s'mores, the most delicious of squares.

4. REST

> For the sword outwears its sheath,
> And the soul wears out the breast,
> And the heart must pause to breathe,
> And love itself have rest.
> – Lord Byron –

My across-the-street neighbors hung their outdoor Christmas lights right after Thanksgiving. I was still in autumn-harvest mode, so it felt a bit too early for me. But my son and daughter-in-law also decorated their house for Christmas that weekend, and for good reason. She's a manager in retail, working at a mall, so if she decorates at home early in the season, she has at least a few minutes to sit and enjoy a bit of holiday peace before she gets caught up in the melee of shopping season and all the work hours it requires of her. In spite of cards and carols announcing "Peace on Earth," we're often personally overwhelmed and anxious during end-of-the-year holidays. But "the heart must pause to breathe." Take a pause to rest. Linger with it. Breathe.

5. A HAWK

> Joy, with pinions light, roves round
> The gardens, or sits singing in the trees.
> – William Blake –

A hawk has landed on our deck rail. I think he's an immature. Maybe a Cooper's hawk, although they're uncommon in the city, but this bird matches the picture of the Cooper's hawk in my bird book. His long tail is brown with broad black horizontal bands and one white band at the end. He sits for longer than I expect him to, turning his head as if to show me the sharp, curved beak of his impressive profile, an angle that says don't underestimate me. He's a stern-looking bird, a predator, and I'm sure he's waiting to see if a foolish finch or a careless cardinal will venture toward my birdfeeder. But my songbirds are savvy; they stay hidden, and soon the hawk takes flight, pinions outstretched. Pumping his wings, he gains height and soars out of sight.

6. IN THE DARK

Faith is taking the first step
even when you don't see the whole staircase.
– Martin Luther King, Jr. –

If I count the sixteen steps of the staircase, I can walk upstairs in my house in the dark. The first time I did it and realized that I actually couldn't see the steps, I shivered at the thought of what I couldn't see. What if the stairs weren't there? What if they ended at nothing, a space, an emptiness? I would step right off. But I kept stepping up, met a solid wooden stair each time, and made it all the way to the top. I know that if I walk in the center of the stairs, they'll creak. If I hug the wall and walk on that side, only the fourth step from the top creaks. At times, I've actually stepped over the fourth step, skipping the creak in order to avoid waking a sleeping baby.

Walking in the dark makes me wonder what senses perk up when I don't see with my eyes? What do I sense in the dark?

7. RIBBONS

> The road was a ribbon of moonlight
> over the purple moor.
> – Alfred Noyes –

I wrapped a package today in paper that was a bright mix of colors. I tied it with red curly ribbon, which works better than stick-on bows for gifts to be sent through the mail. Turning curly ribbon into corkscrew curls is a tactile experience—the feel of the ribbon gliding between my thumb and the scissor blade; the soft scraping, fizzy sound it makes as it slides past; the festive look of a bouncy bouquet of colorful corkscrew curls.

Now I'm noticing other kinds of ribbons, like slick ribbons that catch the gleam of lights, satin ribbons with their softness and sheen, and store-bought bows with ribbons that loop in arches. But there are other kinds of ribbons, like the ribbons of rivers and roads crisscrossing a map or snaking across a real-life landscape viewed from a bridge or a mountaintop or a jet. Rivulets of rainwater ribbon down windowpanes, sidewalks, and driveways—and across my basement floor during a heavy downpour. Ribbons of vine weave in and out of the diamond spaces in my chain-link fence.

Pause and linger a moment when you spy a ribbon today.

8. EVER GREEN

Evergreens are having their moment in this season. Now that other trees stand skeletal and leafless, evergreens show off their winter wear. Pines are fringed with clusters of needles. Spruces wear needles that feather out from their twigs. Fir needles spike out like the teeth of a comb. Cedar branches are flat and scaly. The evergreen holly in my neighborhood has spiky, shiny, dark green leaves and red berries. Then there's the faithful Southern magnolia with its thick, glossy leaves. It's evergreen too. When I moved to Tennessee from Texas, I was surprised to discover that magnolia leaves have long been a holiday decoration here.

In this season of evergreens, I'm pausing to appreciate green. From gray-green to gold-green to dark forest green, it's the color of quiet energy, the color of persistence and patience, the color that connects the year that's passing with the year to come.

9. IMAGINE

> Why, sometimes I've believed
> as many as six impossible things
> before breakfast.
> – Lewis Carroll –

I walked one of my favorite trails at the local botanical garden today. The trail passes among trees where roots vein out across a ground carpeted with moss. I can imagine a fairy world existing out of sight under the cover of low-hanging branches, and I almost expect to see fairies come dancing across the moss along this trail. Imagining, believing impossible things, takes noticing to the next level. The wonder is that sometimes the impossible becomes possible. I can imagine peace on earth. For everyone. Not only can I imagine it, but I can believe in it. And not just before breakfast. I can imagine it, I can believe in it, I can work toward it.

Imagine peace today. Linger with it. Believe in it. Become it.

10. HANDLES

A large, spring green mug sits on my desk holding pens, pencils, a pair of scissors, markers, and a short peacock feather from the decorations at my older son's wedding reception. I've been lingering with it this morning, noticing the curve of the lip, the reflections of window light along the side, and the handle. It's shaped like the letter D. I think I've never really appreciated the simple existence of handles: door knobs, round and cool in the palm or fancy handles curving out like a bridge with a thumb latch; inset handles to open a file drawer; vintage U-shaped drawer pulls that hang down but flip up to open the drawers in my vintage bedroom dressers.

Notice the shape and feel of the different handles you use during the day. Doors, drawers, cups, teapots, baskets, bags, boxes, refrigerators, microwaves, cars. Pull, push, twist, or flip, what would we do without handles?

THE CLIMB

My preschool grandson and I have a running debate about upstairs, downstairs, and the basement of my two-story house. I call the ground level the first floor. Upstairs is the second floor. No, he corrects me, the basement is obviously the first floor. The ground level is the second floor, and the upstairs is the third floor. That makes sense even though it's not quite right. But he's going for the logic of it. I haven't yet broached the subject of first story and second story, because story is what's in books, of course.

When we first thought about buying this house, I considered the two stairways. I wondered if they would become a hardship if we lived here long term. I decided that stairs would keep me in shape. Long term has now arrived, and so far, so good. But more and more, I notice the actual physical sensation of climbing. My legs feel it more and my knees sometimes protest. Still, it's not a bad thing to linger in the climb and notice the push and lift of legs, the feel of the rail under my hand, the shape and feel of the steps. In fact, it's a distinct pleasure to linger with the way the light and shadow angle across the stairs or flow down them like a waterfall. (And while the lower stairs may seem like they lead down to the first floor, they actually do lead to the basement.)

12. THE CYCLE OF BREATH

Sometimes the most important thing in a whole day
is the rest we take between two deep breaths.
– Etty Hillesum –

I'm lingering with my breath at the moment, a practice of slow breathing that emphasizes a long exhale to empty my lungs before taking a full deep breath. I often think of the cycle of breath in a poetic sense. Poet David Whyte describes the cycle as receiving on the inhale and giving on the exhale. Poet Muriel Rukeyser suggests, "Breathe-in experience, breathe-out poetry." I once had a watercolor teacher who suggested thinking about breath in colors. Inhale yellow and blue. Exhale green. Inhale blue and red. Exhale purple.

One ancient word for breathing is *inspire* or *in-spirit*. Inhaling is in-spiriting. So breathe into yourself inspiration. Breathe out your unique treasure of a self. Breathe into yourself love and hope. Breathe out to the world peace and grace. Receive as a gift the pause, the rest between your deep breaths.

13. Music

> After silence
> that which comes nearest
> to expressing the inexpressible
> is music.
> – Aldous Huxley –

If you listen to music, pause with one of your favorite songs. Let the music surround you. Think of the actual sound waves vibrating the floor and walls, vibrating your ear drum, vibrating on and through your skin, filling the air so that you breathe the music into your lungs. Linger with it a moment before moving into the next song or into the next task of the day.

14. TWILIGHT AND GOLDEN HOUR

Sunrise was golden today, a bright flare between trees to the east, silhouetting the tangle of branches against sun-yellowed clouds and the bright blue sky peeking between them. This is the darkest time of year. At Winter Solstice, there's about three hours and seventeen minutes less daylight than there was at Summer Solstice. In my part of the world, the sun rose today about seven in the morning and will set around four-thirty in the afternoon. I only recently learned that each day has two twilights: a morning twilight as the sky grows lighter before sunrise and an evening twilight as the sky grows darker after sunset. I also learned about golden hour, sometimes called magical hour. That's when daylight is soft. (It's a good time to take outdoor pictures.) Morning golden hour happens just after sunrise and evening golden hour happens just before sunset.

Where does the sun rise for you? Over trees? Over plains? Over buildings? Where does it set? Linger with one of the twilights or one of the golden, magical hours.

15. STEPPING OUTSIDE

Sap cheque'd with frost and lusty leaves quite gone,
Beauty o'ersnowed and bareness everywhere.
– Shakespeare –

As I step outside my door today, I glance around to see how the scene has changed from earlier this season. The air is crisper, nippier but not freezing cold. In fact, it's exhilarating. Energizing. The still air is tinged with a drift of smoke, probably from a neighbor's fireplace. The leaves on the mandevilla vine are droopy now, but with the sunlight coming from behind them, they glow yellow around their rust-orange veins. In fact, all the leaves still on their stems are either a crackled, dull brown or they glow in the sunlight. The squirrels are still snooping around too. One is burying some new find. What interests you when you step outside today?

16. CHORES

Tomorrow is recycling day. I gather a week's worth of papers, cardboard, clean cans, and washed plastics out of their indoor holding bin and transfer them to brown paper bags from the grocery store. Usually, I swoop through this task, but today, I decide to slow down and tune in to the moment, to linger with the chore. I listen to the paper rustle and feel the different weights—the light, floppy newsprint of grocery ads;

stiff manila envelopes; crinkly packing paper; smooth printer paper; thick, gray egg cartons; thin, gray cereal boxes; heavy brown corrugated cardboard. I listen to the clank of cans and the clack of plastic bottles. I feel their accumulated weight as I haul them to the large, green plastic bin on wheels. The rumble of the bin as it rolls to the curb sounds a bit like a jet flying over.

So many chores are sensory moments. Washing, drying, folding clothes. Dusting. Sweeping the floor. Washing dishes. I just have to remember to slow down a bit and call my mind to attention.

17. IN THE EARLY TWILIGHT

What glorious cloud-lands I would see,
storms and calms,
a new heaven and a new earth every day.
– John Muir –

When I look through the window facing my desk, I can see a U-shaped dip of sky between a tall, vase-shaped elm in my yard and a tall, rounded tree—I think an oak—in our neighbor's yard. The sky in this wide dip is always changing. It's nature's slowly scrolling scene of the day's weather, which today was windy, chilly, and rainy. This evening I glanced up from my desk to see the tree limbs dancing in the gusty wind. But it was their backdrop that drew me to pause and linger. The sun had just set, and today's thick rainclouds were moving out, trailing clouds layered in soft colors: a gold swathe at the base with pink clouds across them joining a lavender layer above, which eased into thin alternating streaks of dark and light blue-gray leading up to a dark gray layer on top. The storm thundered past in a gray gown, but her train carries the colors of calm.

18. ROUGH TEXTURES

I have a pair of corduroy pants that I pull out for cooler weather. Whenever I put them on, I rub my hand along the ridges and brush the knap. They're a change from the soft, thinner pants of warmer weather. I think of autumn as a rougher season texture-wise. The softness of flower petals is gone, leaving prickly seed pods and dry stems. Leaves are falling, exposing the rough bark of trunk and branch. The bark was always there, gnarled or scaly or smooth or peeling, but now the showy, leafy part of the tree isn't getting all the attention, so the bark is on full display. Then there's the scratchy, drying grass on the lawn. Brittle fallen leaves. Bumpy logs and twigs gathered for the fireplace. I like autumn. I like the cooler days and the textured sweaters. I like the corduroy.

19. LIKE A HUG

As I walk across my sunroom, I catch a scent of Frasier fir that slows me and nudges me to inhale. The fragrance comes from a candle I bought several years ago for the holiday season. It was a bit pricey, but I couldn't resist, because it brought back the air of holidays past. Not specific memories but the ambience, the pleasure, the gladness, the well-being. The crisp, earthy, woodsy scent warmed me like a hug. How can I not linger? What scent hugs you in this season?

20. PILLOWS

I found a small, downy, pure white feather on my bedroom floor this morning. It's not even as long as my little finger. It arcs gently to one side and is so soft that I can barely feel it in my fingers except for the sharp point at the end of its quill. Once in a while, one of these escapes from one of my aging pillows. I sleep with three of them and have had to re-stitch the seams at times to keep the feathers in. But I treasure my old pillows.

Pillows are an invitation to linger. That invitation becomes a temptation when I need to be gearing up or moving on with my day. Just one more moment to linger, I think. But when I have the time to linger longer, when I can plump my pillows, hug them, rest

my head on them, dream on them, it feels delicious
to me, sometimes even extravagant. What a pleasure
to linger with a favorite pillow.

21. TASTING HAPPINESS

The discovery of a new dish does more for human
happiness than the discovery of a star.
– Anthelme Brillat-Savarin –

I'm sipping a cup of Ethiopia Mormora as I write
this. It's truly a good cup of coffee, hot and smooth
and mildly smoky. My younger son and daughter-in-
law met at a coffee convention when they both
worked in the coffee business. They held coffee
tastings the way wineries hold wine-tastings, and they
taught me how to taste different varieties of coffee, to
linger with the top notes and pay attention to the
flavor as it fades. All of us naturally pause and linger
when we taste a new flavor or a combination of
flavors. This year I've lingered over green tea flavored
Kit-Kats from Japan, tangy but strange dill pickle
flavored popcorn, sweet and yummy watermelon
jelly, an amazing lemongrass chicken rice bowl from
a Vietnamese restaurant, and snappy chili-pepper
coated pineapple slices. I'm smiling as I remember the
flavors. Maybe I've tasted happiness.

22. SOLSTICE

On this warm December day
just after solstice,
the sky is restful,
layered in hues of gray clouds,
floating hills of islands
with sun-brightened patches between.
They linger and stretch
and slowly give way
to the whisper of winds higher up in the sky
that foretell icy rain and snow flurries.
But for now, the winds that hug the earth
still hold a trace of warmth.
The birds feel it and flock in flight,
racing across the gray strata of clouds.
They cheer each other on,
dive from tree to tree,
pause to gorge on hackberries.
Fall and spring can feel so much alike.
On this warm day, I can imagine
we're easing toward spring.
But I suppose the birds know
where the year is heading,
aware that this warm breath of a day
is the last wave of fall,
not the salutation of spring,
and it's only a matter of time.

How do birds measure time?
In gusts?
In the weight of the air?
In the angle of light?
In the colors of leaves?
In the slight change in coolness,
a breeze that holds a bit of bite?
However it is that they know,
they do.

It's only a matter of wing-beats before the wind
shifts,
flicks feathers,
shudders branches,
loosens lingering leaves,
ripples the chill, sky-gray water in the birdbath.
Birds will be wintering soon enough.
All the more reason to call out greetings,
to flock in flight,
to fill the trees like plump ornaments,
to savor berries.
There will be time to huddle and roost,
to fluff feathers against the cold.
Soon.
Soon.
But not today.
– kh –

23. LAST LEAF

Last crisp leaf shivers
dangling in the frosty breeze.
Don't let go just yet.
– kh –

Our hackberry trees seem to be the last to leaf out in the spring and the first to lose leaves in autumn. Most of their leaves are gone now except for one that I can see from my bedroom window. It flutters like a prayer flag in the cold breeze but hasn't yet let go. Still, the skeletons of the trees are clearly visible. The hackberries are all elbows and crooked arms. Some have "squirrel holes" in the trunks, places at least large enough for birds to nest in. The holes look a bit like eyes on these old trees. I call the hackberry outside my kitchen window Old Man Hackberry. He's gray, and his trunk is wrinkled like the saggy baggy elephant. The palest green lichen clings to him in patches like age spots. He's the tree where that one persistent leaf clings on. But then, maybe I'm looking at it backward. Maybe it's not the leaf who is clinging to him. Maybe it's Old Man Hackberry who is clinging to the leaf.

24. SOMETHING SINGS

[I]n the darkest, meanest things
There always, always something sings.
– Ralph Waldo Emerson–

With most birds, it's the male who sings, but with cardinals, females sing too. Most of their singing is done in the spring and summer months, but the male will sometimes sing in the winter. He carols, "It's your home, it's your home, it's your home, it's yours. Pretty, pretty, pretty." I think of cardinals as winter birds, although they're around all year long. It's just that after the flowers have faded and fallen, the scarlet red of a cardinal stands out. Cardinals fluff their feathers and look puffy in winter weather, so when they perch in the evergreen magnolia, they look like bright, round ornaments.

What sings to you today, literally or figuratively? Maybe it's a friend's voice. Maybe it's something you see or touch or smell rather than hear. Maybe it silently sings to your heart. Whatever it is, pause and linger with it.

25. PEACE

Begin at once to live,
and count each separate day
as a separate life.
– Seneca –

What's the wonder of today? That's the question I'm posing to myself this morning. But I want to pose it to myself every day. What is sacred and wondrous about this one day? I want to be present for it. I want to linger with it. I want to feed my spirit with it. When I wake up and look out my window, I want to ask, *what wonder is waiting for me?*

26. BENT, BROKEN, SCRATCHED

> I have been bent and broken
> but—I hope—into a better shape.
> – Charles Dickens –

On a shelf beside my desk sits a green plastic cylinder about five inches high and three inches across with a hinged dome lid that has a slot in the top. It's a coin bank that friends of my parents gave them at a baby shower before I was born. Everyone put a bit of money into the bank, and my parents saved it for me. The interesting thing about this bank is that the cylinder is made of nine circular sections painted with characters from Alice in Wonderland. And the interesting thing about these nine sections is that they turn, breaking apart the painted characters and mixing them up. To open the bank, you have to turn all the sections so the scene of characters is complete. It's like a puzzle. Over the years, the bank has been opened and closed and cracked and taped, and the interesting coins are now gone.

This green plastic puzzle of a bank is not something I notice often, but when I do, I linger a moment and marvel. Probably no one at that party envisioned that almost seventy years later that plastic bank would still be around. It's now one of those bent, broken, scratched things that has become a treasure. It has spanned my lifetime and now seems to symbolize the bends and breaks and scratches that come from working out life's puzzles.

27. A WINDOW INTO WINTER

In the depth of winter I finally learned
that there was in me an invincible summer.
– Albert Camus –

Linger at the window you chose to use as a frame (see January 19). How has the scene changed from autumn? As a reminder: If your view is a nature scene, let it be a sacred space, a small revelation of nature. If your view is a building or other structure, let it be a small tribute to shapes, textures, and shadows. Either way, it's a unique view just for you.

28. INTERLUDE

Silence is more musical than any song.
– Christina Rossetti –

Sleet began falling yesterday morning as the temperature outside dropped into the teens. By afternoon, the sleet had turned to snow, and this morning I woke to a silent world blanketed in white. It's now midday, but everyone seems to be staying indoors, and the quiet continues. At the end of a busy, noisy week, this interlude of stillness and peace is welcome.

Linger with silence. Or as Rumi said, "Let silence take you to the core of life."

29. LINGERING WITH THE YEAR

> I myself almost don't know which season I like best;
> I believe all of them, equally well.
> – Vincent van Gogh –

As the year draws to a close, I find myself lingering with thoughts of the past seasons, with memories of what I paused to see and hear, smell and taste and touch. What bubbles to the top of my memories? Trees and skies, I think. I enjoy watching them change from day to day and season to season. I agree with Van Gogh. I like all the seasons equally well.

30. A Marker

Leafless branches arch,
angle, interweave to frame
cloud veils spun of ice.
– kh –

The tick of the clock on my bedroom shelf. The rush of a jet fading as it travels the icy winter sky. The quiet shiver and sway of vines in the chill breeze. This is my present moment as, once again, time carries us toward the speed bump between one year and the next. That speed bump is always a marker of sorts, a chance to glance into the rearview mirror at the year falling quickly behind us before the new year carries us full speed ahead. Thanks for joining me in this past year of lingering. Thanks for sharing your eyes and ears and all your senses. Thanks for opening your heart to the present moment.

This present moment is where peace starts—in the here and now, in my eye and yours, in my ear and yours, in my heart and yours. As much as we'd like to wave a wand over the entire world and make the jumbled and jagged pieces smooth out and fall into place, peace has to start with each of us being peace for everyone we meet.

31. STEPPING INTO A NEW YEAR

Winter welcomes,
beckons,
invites us to
pause
on the brittle brink of the year,
witness
the shimmer of the season,
listen
for undertones of time passing
on icy tiptoe,
breathe
the crisp air.
Drink all of it.
Deeply.
Deeply grateful.

– kh –

This season shimmers. It shimmers with the tinsel and glitter of celebration. But it also shimmers like a mirage, because looking ahead, there's no clear outline. Linger with the unknown, with questions, with anticipation, with the promise of good to come. Linger with hope.

One Last Word

"I like living. I have sometimes been wildly, despairingly, acutely miserable, racked with sorrow; but through it all I still know quite certainly that just to be alive is a grand thing."

– Agatha Christie –